SMALL TOWN
BIG
MONEY

ENTREPRENEURSHIP AND OPPORTUNITY IN TODAY'S SMALL TOWN

COLBY WILLIAMS

Copyright © 2018 by Colby Williams

First edition 2019.

Book design and layout by Rodney Atchley.
Author photo by Mark Neuenschwander.

LCCN: 2018911830

ISBN 978-1-7327810-2-3 (hardcover)
ISBN 978-1-7327810-0-9 (paperback)
ISBN 978-1-7327810-1-6 (ebook)
www.smalltownbook.com

CONTENTS

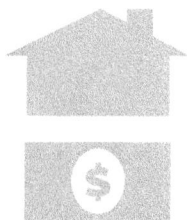

PART I
ENTREPRENEURSHIP IN TODAY'S SMALL TOWN

I AM AN ENTREPRENEUR

I set out to write a book for other small town entrepreneurs like me. Writing a book is a big challenge and getting one published is bigger still, but all of those hurdles could be jumped later. First, I would simply write – not think about the fame and the fortune until the book was written and ready to change the world – just write.

I wrote for three minutes straight, although another half hour passed before I realized how sidetracked I had become. I was working on the book, but I was not writing. Instead, I already had all of the fame and the fortune worked out. My calendar contained a meeting with a nonexistent publisher one year from the day, my friends all knew every detail of my new project via text messages, a dozen relevant economic development agencies received advanced sales requests, and my daydreams included me holding a comically sized royalties check.

This proved to me, if not to anyone else, that I was as ready as anyone to write this book. I am an entrepreneur.

I own a coffee company in a small town – Parengo Coffee of Sikeston, Missouri. It is a small business. It is a small business, but I am not a small business owner. Like I said, I am an entrepreneur.

A frank-talking and rarely-smiling man explained the difference to me over dinner a few years ago. Early in 2015, I had one of those memorable nights which are often so hard to remember. I got to eat a wonderful meal at the late, great *Purloo* in New Orleans as part of an entrepreneur fellowship event, courtesy of the Delta Regional Authority, the federal agency tasked with developing jobs and industries in the 252 counties along the southern portion of the Mississippi River. I had just spent three days trying to keep up, surrounded by some of the brightest entrepreneurial minds I had ever met. Pitches to investors, pitches to pitch coaches, pitches to other pitchers, seminars, key-note speakers, and all the charm New Orleans could muster – by the last night, entrepreneurship was life. So, I'm tucked into a long table with cocktails and course after course, indulging in Chef Ryan Hughes' pickled okra, green tomato chutney, house-cured lamb, and the most insane cornbread I'll ever encounter, and floating in a swill of positive vibrations. With all of this buzzing through my humid brain, the man next to me hit me with an idea that changed my paradigm. I can't remember his name or his face, and the worry that he was some kind of New Orleans Bingo Pajama hallucination has crossed my mind. He seemed very wise, either way. He told me, "Entrepreneurs can be small business owners, but small business owners can never be entrepreneurs. Once you decide which one you want to be, you'll act differently."

An entrepreneur believes he can get stuff done. Many people work hard, but an entrepreneur wonders what would happen if she worked a little harder. Like Walter White, a bad guy on a great TV show, we are not just in the money business; we're in the empire business.

Small business owners continue while entrepreneurs change. Small business owners have a job and a life while entrepreneurs have only one of those and both at the same time. Where a small business owner owns a coffee shop, an entrepreneur owns a coffee company. One is not better than the other. It is not a competition, and it is not just semantics. It is a mindset, and understanding the difference is vital to 1) understanding yourself if you're an entrepreneur or 2) to understanding those empire-minded people with whom you're forced to work. We can be kind of a handful.

THE OPTIMISM BIAS

Entrepreneurs suffer from what experts call "The Optimism Bias." You tell us the odds are one-in-a-million, and our brains translate that to Jim Carrey's voice, "So you're tellin' me there's a chance." We think that even when everyone else fails, maybe we won't. When we have any idea, it is a great idea for at least a few seconds.

We have to wade through this bias, but we also prosper from it. When we are right, and because we were ignorant to failure's wide embrace, we are really, really right. Those with The Optimism Bias are the ones who take us to Mars, cure diseases, reconcile old friends, sail across unknown seas, invent microchips, and show the world what's next again and again.

During my first year with Parengo, each month was a surprise. I wrongly predicted every trend. I am an everyday coffee drinker, and I have a decade of experience, so I thought I knew everything. Others in my town were not as habitual in their imbibement and were new to the café thing. Coffee shops are often a slave to the weather. We were too, but in the completely upside-down direction. Sure, when Fall suggested Winter, everyone expected pumpkin and peppermint, but in the warmer days when I planned to sell a lot of iced drinks, we would be backed up with orders for hot, drip coffee. Then on rainy days when I thought our café would be full of espresso sippers staring out the windows and writing screenplays, instead, we were completely dead.

That first February scared me. Missouri got snow, then ice, then snow again, then a blast of heat, then more ice.

The streets got messy, and my business slowed to a crawl. After I had done as much shoveling and salting as I knew how, I waited. And I waited. Whole days went by during which I brewed cups only for my parents. Toward the middle of the month, I got lonely and wondered how else I could better use my time. Valentine's Day set its Hallmark fangs in deep, and snow days led to thoughts of hot cocoa and sweaters and someone with whom to share it.

My imagination locomotive went down this track:

"I wish I had someone to send flowers to."

"I wonder if anyone will send flowers to me?"

"Wait, guys don't get flowers!"

"What do guys get?"

"There's nothing for guys on Valentine's Day?! What a rip-off!"

I happened to be eating lunch meat at the time. Thus was born my million dollar startup idea: MeatFlowers. com. You fold deli cuts of meat into the shapes of roses and lilies, tie them around beef jerky stems, add bacon just because, wrap it all in butcher paper, and deliver the bouquet to the man who will henceforth love you for the rest of your life! This was the best idea I had ever heard of, seen, or read about. By that afternoon I was ready to give up coffee forever. I wrote a business plan in minutes, traded equity to a web designer, and planned my exit strategy to include a sellout to Edible Arrangements.

This is the Optimism Bias. MeatFlowers is a terrible, terrible idea. In the moment, though, I knew there was no way it could fail. Even those who told me it was stupid received my silent judgment. They wouldn't know a good idea if it slapped them with big, floppy flowers made out of meat right in their faces. Thank goodness I came to my senses. However, if you'd like to prove me wrong by way of proving the old me right, feel free to steal MeatFlowers.com and give it a go. I only ask that you send me a bouquet so that I may feel simultaneously vindicated and infuriated. And because I really like bacon.

ENTREPRENEURS VS. SMALL BUSINESS OWNERS

A small business owner gets content. Or at least contentment is achievable. He's already put in the work to establish a foothold in his community, perhaps even in his industry at large, and then the menu never changes. And that's OK! Stability and consistency are what his customers want. It's what keeps grandfathers bringing grandkids back to the same booth for the same milkshake for generations. It's enough, and it's commendable.

This book may not be for the Small Business Owner. This is for the misunderstood, misfit, renegade entrepreneur who feels like she is the only one who "gets it" in her small town or neighborhood. She sees every sign, park, ad, and street corner and dreams up 50 ways to make them better. She is not alone.

I polled friends in an attempt to organize my thoughts into helpful chapters for small townies like me. I asked questions like:

"If money were no object, what type of business would you start?"

"If you could move to my town and do anything as long as it added value to the community, what would you do?"

And: "What advice would you give small town entre-preneurs?"

To my surprise, normal people do not think thoughts like these. I received answers like:

"I would never start a business."

"I would never move to your town."

And: "Lost phone who dis"

I was shocked! How can people just *be?!* My trashcan sees more ideas for new businesses every day than an episode of *Shark Tank*. If I have a busy morning but a dull lunch, I'm ready to start something new by dinner.

One friend responded, "When I think about start-ing a business I get so stressed out, because I don't even know where to buy a cash register." This book assumes that you're an entrepreneur, or at least entre-curious, and that buying a cash register is not an obstacle that would stop you. If you too are hung up on the register conundrum and were hoping this book would uncover such mysteries of the business world, I encourage you to keep reading, but check out the great work "Where to Buy a Cash Register in 10 Easy Steps & Other Secrets the Top 1% Doesn't Want You to Know!"

For those about to take the plunge or for those in the grind every day who need a little inspiration and maybe a few ideas, this book is for you. In my town, we used to have a magazine. It was assembled by a collective of entrepreneurs in an attempt to rebrand our neighborhood. In the first issue, the Letter from the Editor laid out our manifesto: "Here a group of eager entrepreneurs have decided to do things a little better. These are the crack of dawn, stock the shelves, smile all day, sweep and mop, stack the chairs, and do it again kind of people. They believe *our town can be whatever we want it to be* and that '*because that's the way it's always been done*' is no longer an acceptable excuse."

That spirit took me on a journey. You might be ready to set out too. Before you do, here are things I've learned along the way, as well as lessons from others who have done far more than I have. I hope you find some motivation, inspiration, and just enough perspective to get you where you want to go.

WHAT IS A SMALL TOWN?

Before we get too far, we should define a small town. I hesitate to put a population limit on the term for our purposes in this book, because I think entrepreneurs in some neighborhoods in New York City or suburbs around the Los Angeles area could find value and similarities in these stories and tips. However, for the most part, I am using "small town" to describe towns with fewer than 100,000 people.

These towns are generally positioned away from cities and major airports by at least an hourlong car ride. Small towns often take pride in a single historic building, event, or business. They often have "city limits" signs that boast the years their high school softball teams won their Class A State Championships. Some small towns remind us every chance they get that a celebrity grew up there.

Sure, some towns with 70,000 people operate in a way that is totally dissimilar to what is described within these pages. Also, tiny towns of 8,000 might be right next to a larger community and may not fall within this scope. However, any town or neighborhood that feels a social or geographical isolation - a sense of "we're out here on our own" - may see itself here. This book is for you.

CHAPTER TWO

THE SMALL TOWN TODAY

NOTES FOR THE
OUT-OF-TOWNER LOOKING IN

Small towns across America are ripe for entrepreneurship. Like the Internet, Space, the Wild West, small towns are a frontier which should be considered categorically by opportunity-driven dreamers and considered right away. Up front we can acknowledge the obvious drawbacks to launching an empire in a small town: low population, lower standards of living, lack of potential key demographics for many industries, missing skill sets in the labor force, no venture investors, limited options in logistical channels, and it is hard to explain where the town is located to the unfamiliar. These are generalizations, but many of us must face a portion of these. However, where others see shortcomings, entrepreneurs see opportunities. Plus, once these issues are worked out, we discover this: the small town of today is not a dusty, backward Route 66 fill-up stop that boasts

America's largest autographed photo of Rock Hudson. Today's small town is well-adjusted for the 21ˢᵗ century, and for the right person with some patience, business can be very good.

By and large, our physical space has not changed in decades. We have every fast food option. We have a buffet or two with packed parking lots and giant exhaust fans spewing an invisible cloud of carnival smell across town. We have Tex-Mex out the wazoo and various forms of glazed chicken nuggets with fried rice. We have Wal-Mart for clothes, Wal-Mart for groceries, Wal-Mart for oil changes, face wash, spray paint, guest towels. We might have a JC Penney, a Lowe's, and a CVS. Then we have 100 small businesses in far fewer categories, and that's the way it has always been. This roughly describes my town, and it roughly describes every town. It's all just the same as it used to be.

Notice, however - the _people_ are different. People in small towns are *not* the same as they used to be. At one time, everything was up to date only in Kansas City, and an enterprising young Oklahoman had to travel there in order to find out what was going on in the world. Not so today. Small town people have Facebook. We watch Netflix. If a tweet is read in Seattle, it is read here too. We receive the world's newspapers on our phones every morning, and by the time Saturday night rolls around, we get every joke on *Weekend Up-*

date. Baristas in my shop "just can't even" every bit as much as baristas in yours.

The point is this: we want more. Once upon a time, we had what we had and that's all that we knew. Now we know what's out there, but we don't have it nearby. That's an untapped well for the entrepreneurial mind. In the Pleasantvilles of last century, trends originated on the coasts and moseyed our way twenty years later. Now, social media brings them in milliseconds. Next, trends will begin here (notice the Carhart craze in Brooklyn a couple of years ago). Small town entrepreneurs will be on the front lines when that happens.

We love our towns, our families, and our friends, so we never plan to leave. At the same time, we are more plugged in than ever. Small towners know what brands to wear but have no place to buy them. They've seen gorgeous boutiques and chic cupcakeries and niche food trucks and highbrow temples to mixology. We consume storehouses of style every day in the form of tiny square photos or streaming 1s and 0s, yet the options available to us to spend our money locally are the same as they were for our parents and their parents before them. The Formica countertop is still chipped in the corner, and the plastic booths are slick from the polish of a million denim butts.

Sikeston, Missouri is a good example. We have one of those World's Best Places to Eat Until You Drop Dead restaurants that brings in tourists by the busload. Our Jaycees are very active, with a huge rodeo and other blow-out events. Our factories ship around the world and employ hundreds, and all are decked out in red and black for a Friday night football game. Still, the refrain is constant, "There's nothing to do here."

Fifty years ago, there was plenty to do. The town pulsated at the center – Downtown. Those who remember paint the scenes in Harper Lee style:

"The old piano shop used to be on the second floor right up there, there where Anchor Church is now, right up over there. I don't know how in the world they got them pianos up on that second floor. I think there's still some up there…"

"People in the streets for a concert and the movie theater letting out – I mean you couldn't *get* a car through!"

"The Cotton Carnival was there, right in Legion Park, back then, and the parade would wind up and down the streets around it. I sat there and watched so-and-so and his brother burn their building clear to the ground, and the fire truck had to get in line behind the parade to get to the building. Hundreds of people looking at a carnival, looking at a parade, and looking at a building, watching it burn."

"As a matter of fact, I bet there *are* still some pianos up there!"

It all moved East and South one day, toward the Interstate, the same as it did in your hometown. It kept moving away until the vibrant Downtown shopping district turned into Historic Downtown – an effort to restore the once-great empty shells of buildings and a few stalwart hangers-on, God bless 'em. Decades pass in towns like ours before we realize the strip malls that killed the Downtown are falling apart, the outlet mall that killed the strip malls is hanging on by a thread, and all of our gentry drives to the nearest college town every time they need a latte and a new pair of stilettos. A few faint voices call out for revitalization, but that word is vague, and it echoes through the empty streets.

Then, if we're lucky, the wind changes. Enough people with energy and good ideas decide to go to work at the same time. Millennials get a lot of credit – or blame, depending on your point of view – for giving a second life to classic neighborhoods. Certainly, where would my industry be without the Gen X hipsters before us? But Historic Downtown Sikeston sees few dollars from my generation. In this instance, the time just happened to be right, and the efforts put in by revitalizers of the past decade finally started to pay off.

My parents and I talked about opening a coffee shop. That was as far as we got. I had experience, and they had a little savings. Where? When? What? Good questions. We knew nothing more than "Maybe we should think about doing that." One night I accompanied them to a brand new event: the Fall in Love with Downtown Sikeston Wine Festival. The name says it all, and the next few hours were not what I expected.

When I thought of small towns at the time, I pictured peopleofwalmart.com, so I dressed down. To my surprise, I was the worst looking person on the block. It was a comfortable kind of after-Summer cool, when men can wear sport coats while women can still wear dresses. Twenty bucks got me a wine glass and a handful of tickets, each good for a tasting from one of Missouri's wineries. Their booths lined either side of the street and led to the live music at the far end. In the middle, servers carried mounds of hors d'oeuvres out of Susie's Café & Bake Shoppe, a local staple. Hundreds of people congregated in fours and fives across the original red brick street beneath a canopy of patio string lights and one of those magic hour skies that never quite goes dark. At some point, sitting at a table full of 70-year-old Southern Baptists, enjoying the air and the laughs, admiring our collection of empty bottles, I thought, "Wow. I had no idea."

Soon after, we began in earnest the process of opening a coffee company just a couple blocks away. That night gave me a glimpse of what I now believe: small towns may look like yesterday, but small town people are decidedly tomorrow. Friends and family questioned our decision. I became accustomed to answering, "Are you sure?," and, "In Sikeston?!" Even some lifelong natives were eager to discourage the idea. But the hunch was strong.

Still, I was walking into this young, impulsive, inexperienced, arrogant – a classically entrepreneurial upstart. I needed someone to curb my laser-beam drive and warn me of failure. Luckily, there are plenty of people happy to tell us why our ideas won't work. If well-intentioned warnings are "food for thought," then small town entrepreneurs should prepare for an all-you-can-eat smorgasbord. During my startup phase and in the company's first few months, I listened to critics of all shapes and sizes. This was not my town, originally, so I wanted to learn all that I could.

I found that most free advice fit into three categories:

1) You ain't from around here, are you?

2) Nobody understands the value of a dollar anymore.

3) I knew your dad real' well.

These are also the three areas in which I have discovered the most inaccurate and outdated assumptions. So, don't let them discourage you from the small town frontier! Let me explain.

YOU AIN'T FROM AROUND HERE, ARE YOU?

If you're an entrepreneur in a small town, I hope this chapter encourages what you already feel. For those entrepreneurs considering the move to a small town, I understand that it can be intimidating. It's easy to assume that the locals possess a stereotypical clan mentality in which it is all about who you know. I'm sure this is still true when running for office or joining a country club, but in most of our fear scenarios, it is misapplied. Sure, I've heard the words – "You ain't from around here, are you?" almost *ver batim* – but they come more from curiosity and a lack of anything else to say than from the desire to offend.

I once went to a St. Louis Cardinals' game with a busload of farmers. Seated next to each other, an elderly gentleman and I fast ran out of things to say. I tried the usual questions – What was my dad like as a young man? How big is your farm? Are you glad you switched back to John Deere? – but we straight up had nothing in common and hardly spoke the same language. I wanted to keep the conversation going, because more than anything, I did not want him to ask me where I grew up. I thought that question always implied that I did not belong. I hate talking about who's in and who's out. Hate it. I would pretend to be an expert on almost any subject just to avoid talking about who's related, how we know each other, and with which one of his grandsons I went to high school. I assumed, as a business owner who wasn't from around these parts, that when he figured out that I did not belong and word traveled that an out-of-towner was trying to open up a coffee shop, everyone would boycott on some type of principle. As soon as that type of talk comes up, I shut down. But I could only keep up the small talk for so long. Soon, we fell into an awkward silence. Finally, after a pause which lasted about 25 miles, he asked me, "You didn't grow up down here, did you?"

My worst nightmare, right? Except, that was the end of it. I was still on the trip, one of the guys, going to cheer on "our" team, son of a guy who was son of a guy this guy had heard of, which means something, I think. I assumed that when I answered, "Nope," I'd get thrown off the bus or locked in the bus bathroom until St. Louis, but instead, we just continued not having anything to talk about, and he moved on to talk to someone else. That was it. A local, 60-year-old, millionaire landowner and I didn't want to be best friends. Shocker. Not the end of the world.

As a quick tangent, let us ask ourselves why small town folks might be wary of out-of-towners with big plans for their towns. Consider the man's point of view. Small towns across the map, like I said at the top of this chapter, see progress and abandon in spades. A large company comes to town and wants to build an outlet mall and promises millions in tax and tourism revenue. They get everyone excited about it. City leaders make concessions for them, and landowners are persuaded to sell their prime real estate at a bargain for the good of the community. The mall promises jobs and growth. Then a few years later, it's a huge spread of concrete and empty windows. Business is not what they thought it would be, so the large company pulls the plug. It happens again with a big box store a few years later and again with a giant grocery chain a few years after that. Eventually, our small towns are pocked with cement scars, which make up tens of thousands of square feet of commercial real estate that no longer does commerce. And who do you think pays when the City is forced to finally bulldoze the rubble or make drastic repairs in an attempt to save the buildings? The people who lived here the whole time are left holding the bills. It's no wonder they can be a little suspicious when we march in like the next big thing. They've been through this before.

When it came time to open Parengo, lenders and patrons couldn't have cared less where I was from as long as the plan, the product, and the service were right. Shying away from a good concept and a great community because I was afraid of not fitting in would have been a mistake. It was up to me to prove myself by showing up every day and building something that could last. Eventually, we become someone who belongs and who is worthy of trust. Plus, something good even came out of that interaction with the farmer. I tried to dress cool for that Cardinals' game, and that farmer's suspicious gaze led me to realize that I was not a V-neck and cardigan kind of guy. It was a phase. I was young. I don't have the build for it. I owe that man a Thank You.

If you, from the outside looking in, let "You ain't from around here, are you?" stop you from the opportunities that small town entrepreneurship affords you, you assume that everyone in a small town is the same. Take one lap around Downtown Sikeston, and this becomes impossible to believe. The director of our neighborhood's development group is a serial entrepreneur, Rush Limbaugh fan, antique collector, and oil painter. He gets coffee every morning and chats with an architect from Washington who owns a pawn shop and a bartender-slash-construction worker who moved here from Southern California and who stars in a viral YouTube video involving a horse and a fence. The barista who serves them practices homeopathy and sometimes wears her hair rockabilly blue. By lunch time, Susie's server is handing menus to a table full of women who love to knit as well as to the guys from the tattoo shop who have yards of visible ink and who never miss the meatloaf special. Passing down Front Street, you'll see just as many soccer mom Suburbans as you will sporty two-doors, trucks with lift kits and extra loud exhausts, and laid-back sedans with tinted windows and large, shiny rims.

About seven months after opening, we decided to try to host an Open Mic Night. Nothing new – every bar in every town in the world has one. Except Sikeston. There hadn't been a regular venue in Sikeston for a great while. We asked two talented regulars to host the event with the understanding that if no one else came, they would play for an hour or two for free drinks. Since there is no Scene (with a capital S) to impress with rehearsed material, they were just glad to get out of whatever basement they were sleeping in at the time.

Stereotypes may begin as truths sometimes, but they spread long after they cease to be true. A certain stereotype lingers around small towns – the one that says different is bad. Just as much as the stereotype may keep some out, it keeps others locked away, thinking they don't belong, dreaming of escape one day. That night, possibly for the first time, those who felt different had a place to go. Out came the weird and the stragglers, the bearded and flannelled, the bloggers and vloggers and wannabes and youth ministers. We suddenly became the Lady Liberty of all businesses open past the time when the streetlights come on. A 30-year-old man played his guitar in front of people for the first time that night. An 18-year-old woman sang as loud as the room could stand. A 68-year-old hermit got out of her house, slowly but surely, for the first time in a long time, just to listen a bit. Someone read poetry. There were ukuleles and iPhone synth apps. The place was standing room only. Who knew?

"From around here" means something different to everyone. Parengo's Open Mic Night ran for years. It would have been easy to assume that no one in a town like this would participate in live music at a coffee shop, but then we would've missed out on the dozens of familiar faces who now consider our shop a second home. We could've believed that the local pool of hip kids lacked skill, but we would've missed out on hearing some seriously talented unknowns who now gig all over the place. The Open Mic Night crowd was "from around here" as much as anyone is, and now, at least to them, being "from Sikeston" means getting to play your songs Downtown at the coffee shop and receiving applause for it.

The assumption that one must be a Somebody from a small town in order to launch a successful enterprise also implies, at least in part, that local successes grew their companies by having an acceptable last name and not from hard work or business savvy. It does a serious injustice to people like Adam, chef and owner of The Glenn in Charleston, Missouri, who brought low country cuisine and classical technique to Missouri's Bootheel. He did it by working his way up through kitchen lines between here and the Pacific Ocean – not because of who he knew. Now he puts out the best shrimp & grits in the Midwest. Likewise, the name

Walton means everything now, but it didn't start out that way.

Viewing small towns as if their motions are preordained cheapens the struggle for those who deserve respect for what they've built. Don't hide behind the stereotype. It's an excuse. You can overcome it if you put the work in. The small town of today is nothing if not hardworking and not as narrow-minded as you might think.

NOBODY UNDERSTANDS THE VALUE OF A DOLLAR ANYMORE.

My biggest anxiety since the day we opened has been money. We all feel it. No matter what industry you're in, when you go to a trade show or conference, your schedule ends up packed with "Access to Capital" or "Managing Your Payroll" or "Revenue Stream 101." A life of counting pennies is what we chose when we neglected the nine-to-five route.

In a small town, the dollar has more gravity. There are less of them, and they are harder to come by, so we think of money a little differently. The General Theory of Relativity, when adapted, aptly describes how money works in a small town. Replace matter with money and you have it: it takes a lot of energy to make, and it seems to move away from us at the speed of light.

Money people like to speak in percentages, so here is a typical set of small town figures: the venture capital available in my town is 0% of what it costs to open a coffee shop, and the cost to launch a tiny company like mine was 800% of what I made the previous year. That's not a good balance. Taking a leap and investing in a startup is risky no matter where you live, but it is particularly painful here. The value of a dollar changes drastically as one moves from Silicon Valley to Swampeast Missouri.

Years ago, I wanted to be a screenwriter. I read every book and website I could find on the subject, especially those which featured firsthand accounts. I paid attention to the beginnings of each writer's journey, because that's where I was: right at the beginning. How did they get from where I was (sitting on my gross couch) to where they are now (probably on a much nicer couch)? Far too often, the writer told some version of the same story. Something like: "There I was. Dirt poor. Down to my last can of frank 'n' beans. Ready to give it all up forever. That's when my agent and my manager and my best friend, the famous director, and my wife, the studio executive, said to me..."

Hold on. Agent?! This son-of-a-gun already has all of these connections and can't figure out how to write a script?! Stop the whining! I would have given all the frank 'n' beans in the world just to find one book titled *What I Did Before I Got an Agent.* My highest aspirations were to one day reach a point that these writers considered their rock-bottom moments.

Similarly, at the aforementioned New Orleans Entrepreneur Week in 2015, I sat in on a morning (aka poorly attended) session by a techy big-data guru for whom, I'm sure, much respect is due. I hadn't heard of him. This man has probably had to work very hard and has likely earned every penny he's made, but when I had the chance to learn from him, I felt like I missed a semester full of prerequisites. His Great American Origin Story began with he and his buddies as a group of shmoes sitting in a diner with nowhere to turn and only $200,000 in startup capital. By point C or D chronologically, they had a "tiny" fund somewhere in the millions. If you think a company with $200,000 in the bank is the rags part of the rags-to-riches story, you are not from a small town.

In some cities, money for startups flows so freely that even companies that might be fake can strike it rich. One infamous visionary is currently facing criminal charges because authorities suspect that she sold lies for years by playing the Silicon Valley game like a pro. The truth is still a mystery at the time of this writing, and even if true, this is by no means a common representation of anyone in the startup world, but it goes to show how entrepreneurs can find dollars in some places. In small towns, even great ideas may find nothing.

[1] Nick Bilton, "Elizabeth Holmes, Somehow, is Trying to Start a New Company," 2018, Vanity Fair Hive, 13 Sept. 2018 <https://www.vanityfair.com/news/2018/06/elizabeth-holmes-is-trying-to-start-a-new-company>.

Getting started is hard. Longevity is hard. Being financially successful in business seems like a million years away, and it all feels that much more difficult when you live in a town in which a used espresso machine costs the same as a house just five blocks away.

Small town entrepreneurship is risky. Startup costs are pretty much the same no matter where your business lives, but margins shrink in a small town. Wages are lower, so prices have to reflect that. There are fewer potential customers, fewer cars passing by, fewer pedestrians, fewer everything you need.

While on a heater, a large or growing business will overlook small towns as options for expansion. And it should. It is moving quickly and wants to get as big as it can as fast as it can. If you have the money to open anywhere, open on the busiest corner of the busiest city in the world. However, if money is your biggest startup obstacle, then small towns should be on your radar. The big, hot companies aren't coming, leaving thousands who want great products, service, and jobs nearby. That's where you come in.

Social media and television have already helped you create the demand for quality in hundreds of underserved communities. Yes, it is challenging to fill that demand and to do so profitably, but once you finally make a dollar, it goes a lot further in a small town. Property is cheap. Labor costs less. Daily operational costs are often inexpensive. Taxes, entertainment, recreational costs, and even the price of gas are much lower than in nearby cities.

With Parengo, the leases we've been able to negotiate would blow your mind, especially if you're already paying rent on a storefront in a metropolitan area or had to pay a "key fee" just to receive the privilege of paying rent. Thirty miles away our rent would be tripled at least. In the closest large city, it'd be twice even that.

Same with my house. One of my best friends used to serve cocktails in Los Angeles. She took home WAY more money than I do. Even while making good, adult decisions with her money, she still struggled to afford her studio apartment. Here, after about eight months in business, making very little, I bought a house without breaking a sweat. A whole house! Multiple rooms! I pay extra on my principle, and still it's a conservative 50% of any 400 square foot lease agreement in any city with a population of 200,000 or more.

In small towns, those who understand the value of a dollar can get a lot out of them. Surgeons move here to own farms and horses and to live the quiet rancher life. Owning a row of buildings and collecting local art and escaping to a country cabin on the weekends – these are goals a small town entrepreneur can reach in years instead of decades. If these things are attractive to you, don't let the fear of scraping by in the beginning deter you from the rewards of a small town dollar.

I KNEW YOUR DAD
REEEEEEEEEAL WELL.

"Now, who are you?"

I make fun of my mom every day for this question. It's not the same as *What's your name?* or *Have we met before?* In a small town, *Who are you?* is the out-loud version of Facebook stalking, a background check, and a DNA swab sent to 23andMe all rolled into one. We call it "just being friendly."

My family is as small town as it gets. They can fill an entire Thanksgiving dinner conversation by listing names of people they know who recently passed away. To many small town people, this is the way we share our common experience. We knew these people. They were us. We all built this town, for better or for worse, together, and our friends will not be forgotten. But it does take some getting used to if you're not from a rural area.

Small town conversations have a tune and a cadence all their own. You'll notice this in the way a certain generation here gives directions. I might say: "Our new shop is exactly two miles east of here on the south side of the street." But my mom would say: "It's in the old Taco John's building next to the old McDonald's that isn't there anymore in front of the old skating rink. Right by where the bus station used to be!" Shared experience. We lived here through all the changes, and we're changing it still.

Who are you? is like that. We can continue on as strangers conversing, or we could try to find a more common ground. I probably knew someone you're related to or someone you knew down the line. Knowing that, we could trust each other. We're from the same stock. Then we can converse as friends.

These questions are intimidating to out-of-towners, because, one might assume, the wrong answers would bring shame and doom upon hopeful entrepreneurs. However, that's not the case. If you replied, for instance, "I'm no one from nowhere, and I don't know where the old skating rink is, but I just moved here from Chicago and opened a butcher shop around the corner," then my mom would be happy to have met you, would ask all about your business, where you came from, how's your family like it so far, and would buy your steaks for dinner that night. She'd cook them until they were beyond well-done, but she'd tell everyone how good they were all the same. The next day, a customer would tell you, "Oh, Theda over at Parengo told me all about that new butcher from Chicago, so I had to come try you out! What a cute little place!" Soon you'd see familiar nods around town, and folks would start introducing you as The Butcher Shop Guy.

One person in a small town can make a huge splash. Everyone knows everyone, and everybody talks about everything. If your business is worth talking about, word will travel fast.

This works in a small town entrepreneur's favor online as well. When someone posts about you in a small town, not as many total people may see it, but nearly everyone who sees it lives within shopping distance from your store. Quickly, your brand can seem well-established, even if it is brand new.

Be warned, though: if your business sucks, the same pattern works toward your demise. In my short time here, I've seen multiple restaurants come and go before I even had a chance to try them. And I'm a guy who tries new places all the time! Sometimes, if I hear a bad review early, by the time I get an evening free, the new place will already be shuttered tight.

Again, this is just as true with your reputation online. We get a slew of travelers every week who are willing to drive four miles off of the Interstate because they read a good review on Yelp! We only have ten reviews (Yelp! is not popular here), so one 4- instead of 5-star review can make a major difference. That one tiny smudge could make a traveler decide to wait until the next good coffee shop pops up before pulling over (It's a really, really long wait, in case you happen to be passing by Sikeston, MO right now). In a city, you're likely to have more Yelp! users – or Foursquare, Urban Spoon, Trip Advisor, etc. – and that means hundreds of positive reviews can protect your rating from even a dozen displeased patrons.

However, the flip side is: in a city, a business must have something very special in order to get noticed. It's hard to find the absolute best cup of coffee in Denver. Here, it's easy. That's not an excuse to be less than amazing, but the ease of ranking highly online, word of mouth advertising, and the overall friendliness and curiosity of a small town makes getting your message to the market a relative breeze compared to your competitors in urban areas. You have to do the rest.

SO, BRING IT ON

If you're amping up to launch a business and scraping together spare change to pay for it, if you hoped to be scaling by now but feel stagnant in your urban neighborhood, if you're searching for a big idea to breathe life back into your career, then I challenge you to consider a small town, despite the three categories of stereotypes mentioned above. We want your products. We're hungry for your innovation. We're craving your great service. Choose us while we're small, and we'll reap the rewards of growth together.

Plus, you might enjoy yourself. I can see the stars from my backyard. It's Autumn. The rhythm of the marching band *rat-a-tats* through the crisp air while everyone else gathers at the Friday night High School football game. I canoed a nearby river earlier today, and I'm about to roast marshmallows on my patio. My parents just called to say they might stop by. My mom is one of the world's sweethearts, and she loves a good s'more and a laugh. For a hundred miles in every direction the earth grows the food that feeds people around the world. And almost everyone within that radius has tried my coffee. Life is pretty good.

The small town of today is alive, and we're looking for a new breed of entrepreneurs to take us where we want to go. Don't be afraid of the stereotypes. Use them to your advantage.

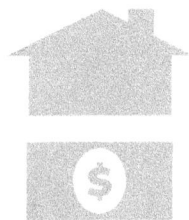

PART II
PREPARING TO LAUNCH

CHAPTER THREE

THE PLAN

One day, after a large assembly of college students, the speaker left the stage, and the lights dipped low. The next two minutes spread goosebumps from the front row to the balcony. Strings and drums brought a video to life – a lone student with a backpack, staring heroically into the horizon. Now he was in the States, now in Europe, now on a train, now in a castle. The orchestra blazed, and the edits grew vicious. The video told of a party. A birthday party would be held. When? Friday night. Other people now. Germans. Czech. Lithuanians. Everyone seemed to be interested in this party. The video's music was in the audience's bones now, and they, too, grew interested in this party. What choice did they have? They *were* the party! They *were* this young man, all as one, traversing the globe to invite the world to a birthday bash. The camera spun around him! *Crash!* "Everyone has heard about it!" *Swell!* "Everyone is ready!" *Spin spin spin!* "And now…is…the time!" *BOOM!!!*

Darkness. The strings stabilized, and the bass reverberated through every clenched backbone. The details of the party grew across the screen, and the music resolved.

Near hysteria, sweaty and mad, as if they'd been holding their breath for a year, every person in the room stood and screamed. They applauded until their shoulders gave out. One lady wept into her lap.

That Friday night, hundreds attended the birthday party. No Europeans could be found, but there was a man dressed like a genie, making balloon animals and with blue-painted skin. There were bands and pizza and *Dance Dance Revolution*. There were horseshoes and volleyball games and a juice bar tended by popular professors. Students entered and exited on a shuttle, which bussed attendees from a parking lot nearby. Every hour on the hour, a hooligan in an inflated cowboy costume burst from the shed, hogtied an unsuspecting partygoer, and gave her or him a t-shirt. They would remember this night for years.

This was my ridiculous twentieth birthday party – mine and two friends born around the same date. We pulled it together with minimal effort, and the total cost to us came to around $30. That night's success can be attributed to one quality: good planning.

I planned that night and its marketing campaign for four months. My friend and I were travelling to Europe that Summer, so I planned the video I would beg him to make. I requested and scheduled it to be played at that assembly weeks before it happened. I drove around town asking for donations of ice, juice, cups, plates, and food. When local managers and business owners heard how many college students I planned to have at my party, they donated whatever I wanted. It was great advertising for them. Several pizzerias donated ten pizzas each and staggered deliveries throughout the night. My friend, Jason, let me talk him into painting himself blue and dressing as The Party Genie. As it turned out, he didn't know how to make balloon animals, and I ended up hosing him off in the backyard and then forgetting to bring him a towel, but that's a tangent we don't have time for here.

I planned every detail and had an idea of exactly how the entire night would go. When it came time to execute my plans, the event seemed easy. My friends and I could relax, play hosts and hostess, and enjoy the music. Plans go awry, and fires must be extinguished, but it's a satisfying feeling when a well-planned event sails by so smoothly.

By the time I launched Parengo Coffee, I knew my brand, developed a great logo and package design, and had rehearsed answers to common questions I might receive across the cash register. I knew the feelings and mood I wanted my shop to convey. I knew how I would train an employee if I ever got to the point of hiring one. We will discuss many of these later, but the point is, I planned every detail. Even though much of my plan never came to pass, and much of it I changed on the fly, the process of planning took away the unknown and helped me learn my own business inside and out.

WRITING A BUSINESS PLAN

Before you launch your business, make a plan. Think through every detail, from how much you will spend to how much you expect to earn to what you want the place to smell like. Picture your business. Picture your first day in business. Picture making a sale. How do you expect it all to work?

Writing a business plan is practically a universal recommendation from everyone who gives advice about starting a company. A classic business plan is a document broken into sections that include demographics, products, prices, and revenue forecasts. Other formats, like Alexander Osterwalder's Business Model Canvas, take the same sorts of sections and make them visual. Instead of typing out paragraphs, you can use sticky notes to visualize how each section works together. Search around and find a template that works for you or check out LivePlan.com for an easy to use online template.

However you decide to make a plan, put time into it. Later we will discuss your expertise in your field, but this is a great time to do research and to learn as much as your noggin can possibly hold. Figure out who your customers will be and whether or not they live in your town. Figure out if you have enough time in the day to do the tasks you think will be required of you. Anticipate how many units you need to sell per day in order to break even. Budget for advertising, maintenance, and electricity. How much does it cost you to make one latte? Would that cost change if you made 200 each day? What if they want it to-go? Research your suppliers, your potential clients, your competition. Putting everything down, whether on paper or on a dry erase board, helps you see how much is involved in actually making your dream into reality. In the process of thinking through everything, you will think of things you hadn't thought of yet.

The other good reason for preparedness is that many bankers, venture capitalists, or partners will want to see your plan. They want to know that you know what you're getting into. They will ask you questions, and you should be able to give confident, succinct answers. Do not use your first meeting with a potential investor or lender as a time to brainstorm and bounce ideas off the wall. When someone asks, "What do you do?" or "What is your idea?" or "Why does the world need this?" be ready to answer in one, two, or three sentences. When you can do that, you are beginning to have a plan.

POINTS TO CONSIDER

As you make your plan, you will begin to master your trade. You will come to know your customers better than they know themselves, at least sociologically. You will discover industry magazines and conventions. You will begin to realize how much hard work this will require of you.

Some valuable lessons must be learned the hard way. Others, however, should be common knowledge, but for some reason, they aren't. Many small business owners and would-be small town entrepreneurs dig themselves into holes that become very steep very quickly. Here are a few subjects, stories, and tips one should consider during the earliest stages of one's plan. Another similar, early-stage subject – branding – has its own section later. For now, think through these:

RESPECT THE CORPORATE VEIL

Your business is you. You conceived it, nursed it to life, embodied it every minute of every day. People yell, "Hey [Whatever you do] Guy!" when you're out in public. You're its face and heart and soul.

But it's also not you. You own it, and you work there. It is its own thing, though.

You have your house, your car, your bank accounts, and your other assets. Set your mind hard on the opinion that these are separate from your business. Your company should have its own checking account, credit cards, or lines of credit. When you buy supplies for the business, the business should pay for them. When you need to pay rent at home, that comes out of your pocket. Keep a line between the company and yourself.

This means you should plan to draw a salary or a wage. If that will not be possible, devise a way to live off of your savings or off of a single income if you are working with a partner. You will be glad you did this. When it is time to sell assets, to pay taxes, to devise a profit and loss statement, or to make almost any major changes, you will be way ahead of the guy who is combing his backseat for receipts and begging his friends for a loan.

Three of my good friends from college started a gym together. They teach trampoline, tumbling, parkour, balance beam, and the whole thing. From the minute they registered their company's name online, they acted dogmatically about keeping everything separate. One stayed working and paid for housing and food, while another lived with him for free, allowing the second one to quit his job and to work full-time setting up their gym. They set a value to this and worked it into their ownership breakdown. When one of them makes a purchase for the gym, he brings a receipt to the next group meeting and either gets reimbursed immediately or adds it into his tally for the next time they draw owners' payouts at the end of a quarter. Their books are spotless.

One day, disaster came calling. The infamous Joplin Tornado of 2011 wiped their gym off the map. The following weeks were very hard for thousands of people. My friends knew the insurance saga would be difficult, and they worried. Would they all need to go back to work? Would they be allowed to rebuild before their savings ran dry? This was their livelihood. But because they kept their accounts so meticulously straight and because they had a well-prepared plan, their rebuild happened way faster than anyone expected. Their brand new, beautiful gym provided a much-needed place of energy and safety for hundreds of kids in the months and years that followed the tragedy. Enrollment skyrocketed, and my friends received a *Phoenix Award* from the Small Business Association that year for rebuilding after a natural disaster.

MIND YOUR DEBT

Goldie interviewed for a job in all three departments of the new Three Bear, LLC. In the Porridge Department, she met Mr. Pappa. He spoke loudly, smoked a Churchill, wore a wide tie thrown over his shoulder, and practiced putting golf balls into a rocks glass on his office floor. He did not ask very many questions. Instead, Goldie listened to Mr. Pappa lecture about how big the Porridge Department would be when he got through with it. He planned to take out loans from every bank between here and Nebraska. He predicted porridge would be the new Tide Pod – everyone would be eating it! In Mr. Pappa's plan, all the debt in the world would not matter, because he expected sales to be high enough to pay it all off within a year.

In the Chair Department, Goldie interviewed with Ms. Mahmah. Her office was very small and painted beige. Her suit and personality can only be described as austere. Goldie found the Chair Department to be very quiet and did not come across any other personnel there. Ms. Mahmah explained that her department had yet to make a sale, but as soon as they sold one chair, she would buy some wood. After the second sale, she planned to buy a saw to cut the wood. Eventually, if sales kept coming, she would be able to purchase all of the equipment required to build the first chair. The sky was the limit after that.

Goldie felt better about the Bed Department as soon as she walked through its doorway. The boss introduced himself as "Junior" and gave her a tour. Work seemed to be progressing in this part of the company. Junior showed her the new hires running a mattress-making machine, which was "a little old but didn't cost an arm and a leg." He showed her around the sales offices and through the section of the production room where the new frame-making machine would go once they hit their sales quota and could secure an expansion loan. Goldie asked about debt. "I took out enough to get us going,"

Junior replied. "But I keep the monthly payment beneath a certain percentage of our monthly sales." Goldie thought that sounded just right.

Most of us do not have hundreds of thousands in savings. In small towns, traditional or SBA loans are often our only options for financing a new venture. We are hungry and ready to grow as fast as we can, and that can get us into trouble. The stories I read about tech startups on the West Coast make be believe that my business should be moving as quickly as theirs. My market is different, though. The traffic I deal in is way less than that in a city. We may reach billions in sales one day, but until then, I cannot suffocate my company in loan payments. Patience is hard to learn but essential in a small town setting.

At the same time, I have to have some money in order to operate! So, finding the right balance for the pace of my business is imperative. Eventually, maybe the cash will be stacked so deep that I can swim in it like Scrooge McDuck and I can pay upfront for everything. Until then, I will work with my friendly, neighborhood banker.

In personal finances, institutions tell us to divide our monthly debt payments by our monthly gross income. This gives us our debt-to-income ratio. Many people feel safe if their debt-to-income ratio is 20% or less. Some say 15%. Some want 0%. Some aim for a number in the 30s. With larger businesses, accountants talk about the debt-to-equity ratio. This is their total outstanding debt divided by all assets. A number less than one is normally good, while more than one is bad. However you and your accountant look at the numbers, make sure your income from sales brings in enough money to make your debt payments while still operating your business throughout the month.

BREAK-EVEN POINT

There is one number you should have in the back of your mind every day. Let's say you make ice cream sundaes. You know how much the cups cost, the spoons, the whipped cream, the hot fudge, the soft serve mix, the sprinkles, and the cherries on top. You figured in how costs increase throughout your smalls, your mediums, and your double-extra-larges. The electricity costs. The labor does too. Cleaning supplies, paper towels, loan payments, and music licensing fees all get added to the number. With everything finally summed up, there is a number of sundaes you must sell every day in order for the profits that are built into every unit to add up to cover your total costs. This is the break-even point. If you hit that mark, on average, throughout a week, a month, a year, or a decade, you will not make any money, but you also will not lose any. Even one peanut sold at a profit over the break-even point puts your company in the black. On the other hand, one unexpected expense moves your break-even number up – meaning you must sell more units per day on average in order to break even.

I know a small business owner (not an entrepreneur) who has no desire to build an empire. He owns a business and cares about it. He works hard at his trade, and he is awesome all around. He runs his business in order to live comfortably, to be his own boss, and to take time off whenever he wants to. His is a totally admirable ambition, even if it is different than mine. He also keeps his break-even point in mind every day. He knows how much he must make per week in order to maintain the lifestyle he wants. Sometimes, by Thursday afternoon, he has had a great week already, so he closes the place and stays home all weekend. That is the perfect life for him, and he affords this luxury by keeping that one number as his goal. You should know your break-even point and aim above it every day.

REVENUE

One might assume that every businessperson possesses an innate sense of how to make money, but it is shocking how many fresh business plans lay out the blueprints for what sound like charities instead of businesses. I judged a local pitch competition recently and I had to ask one participant, "So, do you sell something, or is this a place for people to hang out?" She never came up with an answer. By the end of your business plan or planning phase, make sure you can clearly state _where the money comes from_!

Pretend you own a furniture store. People come in and buy furniture. That's one revenue stream. You also sell furniture on your website. That's a second revenue stream. Maybe you even have a rent-to-own program. Each of these streams compile to make up your answer to "How do you make money?" When you can answer that, you can think about how to increase the flow in each stream.

The primary revenue stream on Day 1 should be obvious in most cases. I opened a coffee shop, so my only revenue stream consisted of selling drinks to customers who walked in the door. Knowing this, I also knew I could increase sales by persuading more people to walk in the door. When I added a revenue stream, it was wholesaling coffee and other products to other coffee shops. I knew I could increase that stream by finding more coffee shops to sell to or by persuading people to open more coffee shops.

Creativity can carry an entrepreneur a long way. I could rent out my shop for events, I could host my own events after hours, or I could provide a catering menu to other places where people host events. I could tweak my wholesale coffee catalogue to include fundraiser options for schools and youth groups, or I could seek out companies who want to offer their own brand of coffee and sell them "private labeling" fulfillment services. I could even rent out the down time on my roaster to another coffee company who wants to start roasting without all the overhead. Some of these things have nothing to do with my original business plan, but all add revenue in diverse ways to my empire.

You could teach classes on your craft, set up a subscription box or membership service in-store, or even sublet half of your space to a completely different type of company. Think of ways to take your business to more people. Think of other ways to make your business scarcer and more exclusive. Each brainstorming session could add another revenue stream and will help you remember that one of your primary focuses is where your money comes from. As long as you're still in the planning phase, you have the freedom to imagine creative revenue streams that branch off of your main offering. Go wild. You may find something which adds little expense and lots of profit.

That same hypothetical furniture store we discussed above could charge a fee to stage homes for real estate photoshoots, or they could rent set pieces out to theaters or to video crews. An art gallery next door to my shop hosts classes in the evenings and brings in well-known painters for weekend workshops. Our town's taco truck proprietor caters events on the side, sometimes even parking the truck indoors when the venue is going for a hip vibe. Many entrepreneurs supplement their main revenue streams by adding Amazon or Etsy stores, sending mobile versions of their businesses to trade shows, or entering into wholesale arrangements with competitors. Others with brick and mortar locations purchase the property which houses their businesses. This turns what once was a rent expense into an asset and provides additional revenue if other residential or commercial tenants occupy the building. Some entrepreneurs build income-generating personal platforms online and set themselves apart as experts in their industries. There's no limit to how creative you can get when dreaming up how to make money in, around, and from your startup.

PLAN FOR GROWTH

Set yourself goals from the outset. When you surpass your break-even point and begin to see a profit, plan to save some for your growth objectives. With a goal for how you will expand or improve things, you can budget for it. If you find yourself with a fat wallet in three years, but you have not considered what to do with it, you may lose momentum. Planning how you might grow from the beginning allows you to snowball your success when it comes.

In corporatespeak, they refer to "Phase 1, 2, and 3" or maybe A and B. These are titles assigned to stages of growth. They plan to roll out expansions and improvements in a particular way based on their research, budget, and speculated sales. That plan can change at any time, but having a plan gives them company-wide goals and defines a group effort.

You may not have a group at the outset, but financiers and customers alike can more easily buy into your vision when you have a plan. Planning for growth can also help you slow down. Do you get overwhelmed because you want to include every cool thing you can think of into your business but don't know where you'll find the money? Whittle it down into the essentials and plan the points at which you will add everything else, a little at a time.

Around age eighteen, I discovered stir fry. Every day after school, I would toss broccoli or bell peppers or chicken or jalapeños or shrimp with whatever sauces or noodles my mom kept in the pantry. I threw in some soy sauce here, some of Emeril's seasoning here, or cracked eggs all over everything. I did not know what I was doing, but it sure tasted delicious.

When I moved off to college, someone introduced me to my first Mongolian Barbecue. While I am certain this is not how they eat in Mongolia, I was ready to pledge allegiance to whomever came up with this idea. I stacked every single option onto one towering plate and waited to receive my award for Greatest Bite of Food Ever Assembled. When the dude in the paper hat slid my plate to me beneath the sneeze guard, it appeared to be all the same shade of brown. No sweat. It'd still taste great. I knew it would. Then, to my surprise, it tasted…just like stir fry. Stir fry and Mongolian Barbecues are still awesome. Don't get me wrong. However, combining every ingredient into one dish is the equivalent of painting with every color all at once.

Years later, I sat through my first tasting menu at a chef-owned and -operated restaurant. Each flavor and texture came out alone and with pizzazz, well-paced, well-spaced, and treated with respect. At these types of places, even if the chef sends out a spoonful of fluff made from orange peel, it is the orangiest peeliest and the fluffiest fluff you've ever tried.

Like the fine dining chef, treat each phase of your business plan in its own way, rolling it out only when the timing is right. Instead of trying to do everything all at once and smearing it all together into your version of mud, plan to grow into each phase of your empire when you can afford to execute each aspect in the best way it has ever been executed. It wouldn't make sense for my nice shop with its white tile and chemistry lab brewing devices to offer terrible cheeseburgers on Styrofoam plates. If I threw together a menu just for the sake of expansion, that might happen. Better would be to know exactly when coffee sales reach the point that it pays to add a kitchen, to hire someone to develop and to prepare a menu, and to advertise our new offerings. You can have everything you want included in your brand if you take the time to make a plan.

INNOVATIVE RURAL BUSINESS MODELS

BY BECKY MCCRAY

Rural and small town businesses aren't limited to the downtown mom-and-pop stores or the businesses recruited into the industrial park any more. In fact, rural businesses today don't really have to look like any of the old-fashioned business models for small towns.

The traditional way to go into business in a small town was to have an idea, try to find a usable building, develop a business plan, create the legal organization, then figure out marketing, staffing, financing, and more. You needed a lot of personal assets, great credit, good connections, prior experience, and maybe even insider knowledge. This put a huge barrier between an entrepreneur's idea and going into business.

The new, innovative models tear down barriers to entry. Today's Innovative Rural Business Models include businesses that incorporate tiny, temporary, together, traveling, and technology. They add up to new ways for more rural people to participate in the potential benefits of owning businesses with less risk of catastrophic failure.

TINY

Expecting one single business to fill an entire building creates a barrier to entry. Divide large spaces up, allowing many different businesses to fill just one tiny space. Others are doing this already.

In Washington, Iowa, there is a business called The Village. The huge old department store building sat empty for decades because no one could fill all 15,000 square feet. It has now been divided up into a little "village" of shops that have only a few hundred square feet to fill. These smaller spaces give a lot more people the opportunity to try out business ideas.

Tionesta, Pennsylvania, had an empty lot where a building burned. After waiting 10 years for a developer to rebuild a full-size building for a single business, the industrial development board decided to try tiny businesses. They put in garden sheds, the big ones that are a few hundred square feet inside and dressed them up with 1800's style false fronts to harmonize with the downtown buildings. The result is called the Tionesta Market Village. All different kinds of people run their tiny businesses inside the sheds. They might never have had the resources or assets to start a traditional downtown storefront, but they can rent a tiny space and get started.

TEMPORARY

Businesses may pop-up for a day, week, or season. Our old image of "real" businesses has them lasting for years, maybe decades with little change. Our new businesses may come and go in a flash as the owners learn something, earn more assets, and gather more fans and customers for their next venture.

Think about booths at events as opportunities for people to test their entrepreneurial ideas and products. Almost every town has special events that could allow booths to include business experiments.

Delaware used pop-ups during the holiday season as a stepping stone to creating new long-term businesses. Delaware Economic Development's Project Pop-up looked for people who already had a following for their business either online or with booths or tiny locations. They selected 18 of the most promising to fill holiday season pop-up stores. Of the 18 selected, 17 went on to sign a long-term lease and grew into full-scale businesses.

TOGETHER

Rural people know how to work together, how to rely on each other. That's why we excel at this model, where separate businesses share a space. Small towns have many examples of stores inside other stores, a business inside a business, as well as co-working spaces, maker spaces, shared studios and galleries, and shared commercial kitchens.

Homewood, Illinois, did seasonal pop-ups during the holiday season, including temporary businesses inside of other businesses. An empanada maker popped up inside a furniture store. Each brought new customers and attention to the other, and both businesses benefitted.

Co-working and maker spaces bring together diverse small businesses to share the assets of a physical location and to connect with each other. Shared art studios and galleries, like the ARTesian Galleries in Sulfur, Oklahoma, extend the sharing and networking benefits to artists.

Commercial kitchens can be expensive to certify and may sit idle much of the time. That's another barrier to entry for traditional businesses. Sharing kitchens can lower that barrier, allowing many new experimental businesses to pop-up. In tiny Dacoma, Oklahoma (pop. 107), the former elementary school building sat vacant until locals converted it into a commercial kitchen incubator. One family brought out their traditional recipe for pickles and used the incubator to launch a now-thriving business.

TRAVELING

Rather than depending on the market in one town only, innovative businesses are hitting the road to round up customers. You're used to seeing food businesses operating out of trucks and trailers, but this idea has expanded. Retail stores and boutiques now commonly operate from a truck or trailer. Service businesses are using this model, too, such as wedding planners and financial consultants. Just about any kind of business could go mobile, so this model appeals to established businesses looking to expand outside their local reach as well as new businesses looking to get started.

TECH-ENABLED

When it came to hiring and being hired, or to finding customers and suppliers, small town people used to be limited to whom they could find locally. Today, technology means we can work with or work for people and companies from all over the world. Independent professionals can make a living from the gigs or work they earn using online platforms. These platforms take very different approaches, but all provide ways for rural people to connect to work they couldn't find without technology. The specialized nature of platforms help skilled entrepreneurs find clients looking for exactly what they offer; some well-known examples of these platforms focus on curating the work of freelance professionals, handmade items, online stores, art, and even book printing.

The flip side is also true, with rural people building successful businesses without ever hiring an employee.

They do it through hiring independent professionals for specific gigs or projects, often using the same online platforms. It's now possible to build a million-dollar one-person business from the smallest of small towns.

HOW THIS SPREADS OPPORTUNITY IN SMALL TOWNS

Especially for rural areas where many people don't have a lot of personal assets or wealth, the traditional risk of ownership may be too much for one person to bear alone. That's why community ownership, cooperatives, and employee-owned models are also appearing. Cody, Nebraska, has a community-owned and student-run grocery store, the Circle C Market. The students even built the building! Now, they run the store.

By removing the old barriers to entry, the Innovative Rural Business Models spread opportunity to many more people. You don't have to have personal wealth to get started. You don't need all the best connections. You don't have to risk everything on a big experiment. You can start small. You can try it just for a day. If you fail, you can recover quickly. If you do well, you can parlay that into a larger try.

ABOUT THE AUTHOR

Becky McCray is a small town entrepreneur – she and her husband, Joe, own a retail liquor store and a cattle ranch. She shares insights from her real-world experience at her highly-ranked website, Small Biz Survival, and in her award-winning book, *Small Town Rules*. Her practical perspective is featured in three books, dozens of newspapers, magazines, blogs, podcasts, and university publications. She makes her home base in Hopeton, Oklahoma, a community of 30 people. Check out her very helpful website at SmallBizSurvival.com.

CHAPTER FOUR

THE PITCH

Business pitches and pitch competitions were aspects of the entrepreneurial-startup world about which I knew nothing before starting my business. Rest assured, you can launch a successful business and build an empire without ever pitching your business to anyone. However, because it exists, and because an entire subculture now lives in constant pitchmode, you should know what it is.

Made famous by the television show *Shark Tank*, the model for pitching probably began with the thought exercise – or maybe someone's actual experience – of being trapped in an elevator with a billionaire investor. You have 30 seconds before the doors open and he or she walks away from you. Here's your chance! So, in 30 seconds or less, you should be able to get the investor's attention, impress her with an innovative and bankable idea, and answer any questions thrown your way.

Even if that scenario never happens to you, you may meet with a partner or your next great employee and need to hit them with a 30 second elevator pitch. If nothing else, preparing this speech and packing all of your ideas into 30 seconds will help you distill your plan to its best parts. You may start with a panful of soil and sift it until you find a nugget of gold.

Other occurrences of pitching happen all over the world in pitch competitions. Even losers in pitch competitions can succeed in business. However, if you are ready and able, a pitch competition can be a great way to test your idea against an audience and a panel of judges. If they represent some of your target market and don't like your idea, then you may need to rethink some things. Also, if the judges are experts, entrepreneurs, or investors and they cannot see the economic potential of your idea, then it's good to know that before you sink your own money into it. On the other hand, if these same people give you some thumbs up, then congratulations! You may have a winner.

Participants in pitch competitions can win money, time with experts, publicity, and other educational opportunities. Competitions typically require a three, five, or seven-minute pitch with a visual aid. They might call them "pitch decks" or "slide decks." This is your business plan condensed into a PowerPoint, Keynote, or other type of digital presentation. Use good photos. Make it easy to understand. Do not read off of the screen. Practice. You never know who may be sitting in the audience. Pitch competitions may open doors or help you understand yourself, and they almost always will introduce you to great people doing interesting things.

A good pitch should include the basics – here's a problem I see, here's how I can solve it, here's who I am and why I'm the best person to solve it, and here's how I plan to make money from solving it. At my first pitch competition, I knew the basics forward and backward. Then my competition threw out some words that I did not know, and all of a sudden, the judges only wanted to hear from them. So, if you have time left in your pitch allotment, think through these issues and work them into your presentation. Beyond your basics, these next sections touch on what investors want to hear.

SCALABILITY

While trying to look poised and impressive in front of a group of people in suits, I once fielded a question on my company's "scalability." I opened my response with a thoughtful head nod, followed by a long swallow, and the obligatory stall line, "That's a great question." I have BS'd my way through too many public speaking engagements to count, so I considered making up a story on the spot that might throw the audience off my scent. However, this time I decided to come clean. I replied, "I don't know what that word means." Everyone laughed.

I'll save you the embarrassment. Scalability is your company's ability to grow or to reach a high volume of sales. When people ask about scalability, they want to know if you have revenue streams that could grow exponentially if only you had the money to make it happen. A great barbecue joint with the world's greatest fresh pulled pork sandwich can be a fantastic business, but it is not particularly scalable. Maybe it only works in that location, with those cooks, on that smoker, or with that local hog. If the same company developed and packaged a tasty barbecue sauce, investors may be intrigued. A sauce could be reproduced inexpensively and sold far and wide. Scalability with the sauce is high.

Without knowing this word, I intuitively planned my business with avenues for scale. Opening a coffee shop costs a lot of money and requires constant attention, maintenance, and management. The overhead is high, and expansion is slow (low scalability in opening multiple shops). Roasting and bagging beans, however, is relatively inexpensive. Coffee beans are sold in stores, restaurants, and online. Eventually, I planned to become a wholesale supplier of cups, lids, straws, you name it. If other shops purchased supplies from me, and if my beans shipped all over the world, the potential for growth became nearly limitless (high scalability in distributing coffee and supplies). Your ability to create scalability is just as good in a small town as it would be anywhere else, and it is a lot less expensive to achieve it.

When I pitched my plan to open dozens of Parengo Coffee shops, judges, investors, bankers, and friends gave me a lot of "good luck"s. On the other hand, when I changed my pitch to become more about the roasting and wholesale operation – I am the only one doing it within 150 miles of my location, the costs of labor, utilities, and rent are way cheaper in my small town than in my national competitors' cities, and my prices beat those of others who have urban overhead – investors' eyes turned into cartoon dollar signs. They wanted to hear that their one-time investment could allow me to quickly turn a huge profit. They wanted to know if Parengo was scalable.

EXIT STRATEGY

As a bored and challenging student, my high school experience involved developing quite a few arch nemeses. Foremost among these was a poetry teacher named Mrs. Winslow. I pretended to like poetry for most of my young life because I wanted to be seen as interesting; but after Winslow's class, I realized that I do not care for poetry one bit. I would like Shakespeare better as a novelist, and I think Emily Dickenson should have gotten out more. Winslow, for some reason, also tried to teach us Stephen Covey's *The 7 Habits of Highly Effective People*. Since he was important to Winslow, Covey became my nemesis by association. I hated the Habits and have neglected to look at that book throughout my life. However, it seems Winslow gets the last laugh. To this day, I think of one particular habit every time I sit down to write a business plan: "Begin with the end in mind." It seems I learned something in that class after all. Until next time, Winslow.

When opening Parengo, I planned where and how I thought the company would grow. Reminding myself to "begin with the end in mind," I asked, "What's the end goal?" Would I plan to keep growing until I had a shop in every city in America? That seems unrealistic in my industry. Would I consider a franchise model? Was there a point of success at which I would simply stop growing and ride the company to my grave?

Great business plans include an end goal or an exit strategy. You might plan to develop a business fit to sell and then start all over again with a new idea. Since you are considering a small town as your launching point, you may be attracted to the idea of hitting a certain size and staying there until you retire. For my coffee company, I thought the most likely positive outcome would be saturating Southeast Missouri and some of the sur-

[2] Covey, S. The Seven Habits of Highly Effective People. (New York: Simon and Schuster, 1989).

rounding states with my wholesale products and then selling to a strong regional competitor like Kaldi's in St. Louis or Intelligentsia in Chicago. I formulated my strategy five or six years ago, and neither of these companies know I exist still, but it gave me a goal to work toward.

During a pitch, investors want to hear that you could make a realistic and sound decision when some type of moment comes that feels like an end. Would you take the company public when it reaches a certain size, thereby losing control? You'd get rich, and you'd make your investors rich, but would you feel sentimental about a board running your baby? Would you sell out if the right offer came across your desk after years of growing your idea into a competitive and profitable enterprise? Do you hope to hire a manager someday, force him to keep your company tiny, and retire to your RV next to a lake? Investors want to hear what end you have in mind so that they can judge your realism and your emotional investment. Some venture capitalists might be looking for a family business to own for generations. Others want to back you because they believe you will grow and sell quickly, making them a lot of money in only a few years. Stay true to yourself, but realize they are in this to make money.

FAILURE

As a society, we are learning to fail. On several fronts, leaders are publicly faced with their mistakes. We are realizing that even when people make egregious choices and hurt other people, the ability to admit fault – to own it – goes a long way toward beginning the slow climb to forgiveness. On the flip side, when someone obviously slips up and then denies it or gets defensive, we shake our collective head.

Not too long ago, it seemed like CEOs could only act tough and be flawless. Today, some vulnerability and a crash-and-burn background story could generate an entrepreneur immediate venture capital. We like that people are trying things, and we no longer mind when people fail, as long as they learn from it and try again.

So, plan for failure, too. Be open about it. By no means should you expect it or chase it or dwell on it. However, before you begin, anticipate what you will do if the worst happens. When investors or bankers see that you are prepared for anything, they will know that you are not simply a dreamer with a golden tongue.

Imagine you are in the audience during a taping of *Shark Tank*. Mike steps into the room and begins his pitch. He's fresh out of high school, where he was the captain of the basketball team, the debate team champion, the class President, and the Secretary at his state's Model UN. He plans to attend Yale this Autumn. His invention, which pulls potable water out of the air, is his very first invention. In fact, he got it exactly right on the first try.

The second contestant, Jerry, is a line cook at the country club in his hometown, where he is not allowed to be a member because of an old misdemeanor on his record. He did not go to college, but for the past 40 years since high school, he has read everything he can get his hands on about science. He loves inventing and tinkering and dreaming of a better world, and he knows we have a water problem on our hands as a global society, so he spends all of his free time trying to develop a solution. Actually, he's presenting the exact same type of invention – a device that pulls drinkable water from vapor. The one he presents today is his 468th version. He spent all his savings on the idea, but he persevered, and as a result, he knows number 468 is perfect.

Wouldn't you jump out of your seat and scream, "*PICK JERRY!!!*"? This guy failed and failed and failed and failed again, but each bump in the road led him to today. You know his invention is tested. The investors know that if they throw money at Jerry to start a manufacturing company, and then tomorrow something terrible happens and all the company's accounts are frozen, Jerry is far more likely to weather the storm than is Mike. People who hit the bottom and climb to the top are a great investment, so don't be afraid to let your pitch audience know how you've struggled to get where you are today.

While we're on the subject, it is worth noting that in a small town, failure can be extra-intimidating. Everyone knows you and knows your family. We already discussed how quickly word travels here. Some of that is gossip. There's an element of *schadenfreude* – a few people will love dishing about your failure. It makes them feel better about themselves. But the vast majority will watch what you do next. Maybe you lose everything, go bankrupt, sell the last piece for pennies - if you aren't afraid to show your face soon after, owning the points at which you went wrong, then a small town is a great place to receive love and support and to start again. As long as you haven't lied to or tricked anyone, and as long as you don't owe money to everyone in town, falling and bouncing back is something to respect. This frees you up to innovate, create, and take risks in your small town without fearing shame. Use that failure for fuel.

CHAPTER FIVE

THE MONEY CHAPTER

Much bandwidth and many pages are devoted to startup funding, because it is singularly difficult to obtain and important to manage. Accumulate too much debt or begin with too little cash, and life will be very frustrating for a few years. Many hopeful entrepreneurs enter the money stage of their process naïve to what awaits them and soon give up altogether when they meet the first round of red tape and paperwork.

My dad tells of a magical time long, long ago when he walked into banks and walked out with money. He started a business with nothing more than a good reputation, a strong back, and a firm handshake. The conversation with the banker would include the weather, the paintjob on his Pontiac, how their families were faring, and then the banker would promise a line of credit to get him started. An hour later, my dad could purchase equipment on that promise alone.

I assumed banks had not changed much in the subsequent 45 years. I brushed my teeth, put on a tie, and then the banker promptly offered me zero dollars. Bankers have little freedom to take risks these days. They want collateral. They want 20% down. They want cosigners making personal guarantees. These are things most small town entrepreneurs do not have.

Because the classic bank loan is now so difficult for startups to obtain, new avenues could offer solutions for those unwilling to give up. We started Parengo with the ol' out-of-pocket, bargain-shopping, penny-pinching method. I was largely unaware of the greater entrepreneurial ecosystem at the time, and I assumed I would have to go it alone. Had I done better research and discovered these other routes, things might have run smoother in the beginning. Check them out:

ESOS AND YOU!

The organizations which exist to service entrepreneurship are legion, and it seems like new ones pop up every day. Some are regional, while others are tied to a city or a neighborhood. Many are called by long names and describe themselves with purposefully vague nomenclature. They throw around acronyms like idk what. Still, many of these agencies can be supremely valuable to those launching new businesses, especially in a small town.

Some Economic Support Organizations or Economic Development Groups specialize in gap lending, matching loans, and supplemental financing. Consider these as options when a bank will not budge. Consider them maybe even as a first option.

After about a year of business, I received an opportunity to open a second Parengo Coffee café. Still, I could not secure a loan without substantial collateral. Luckily, the Southeast Missouri State University branch of the Missouri Innovation Corporation had just moved into the Douglas C. Greene Center for Innovation and Entrepreneurship (That's the MIC at SEMO housed together with the IRIE, the SBA, and the SBTDC. I told you. Acronyms.). They were eager to develop small businesses in the Bootheel, and they contacted me with an offer. A chunk of money is earmarked each year at almost every level of government to be loaned into the small business sector, and we qualified for some of it. By partnering with a local bank and matching its loan, thereby allowing the MIC and the local bank to partially guarantee each other's money, the MIC filled in the "gap" of our remaining financial need and brought down our combined interest rate in the process. As added bonuses, Parengo got major local press coverage for being the guinea pig for this new program, and we met some great friends in the MIC staff and through its network.

Other groups specialize as "incubators" of several varieties. Some train entrepreneurs through rigorous coaching with the goal that they will be able to pitch to investors, *Shark Tank* style. Others offer cheap or free rent to startups in a shared workspace environment. Some offer equipment for industries whose startup overhead is preventative to entry. Some are very hands-on, some trade equity for membership, and some offer a lifetime of mentoring. There are enough incubators out there today (because "incubator" was a buzzword that helped organizations receive grant money over the past several years) that you should weigh them against each other before you sign up for programming or services you do not need. However, assuming you have a great local incubator, the benefits can be substantial, and the value of sharing space, time, and energy with other ambitions creative types is immeasurable.

No one is handing out free money. Inevitably you will hear about grant money for rural businesses. I am telling you up front: those grants do not exist. It is a common misconception. Grants go to towns and roads and nonprofits, but no one is giving grants to private enterprises. Economic Support Organizations are no different. They do grant entrepreneurs valuable resources, nonetheless. Simply meeting other people in your town or region who possess similar wiring is refreshing, especially in a small town when you are few and far between. Too much cannot be said for smart networking in tightknit communities. Calvin Friedrich, a startup academic and an all-around great guy, answered a questionnaire I sent out for this chapter:

"Surveys show that entrepreneurs learn more from other entrepreneurs than any other source. The advantage of small towns is the willingness of community members to be of assistance. Call it Southern Hospitality, Midwestern Charm, or whatever you want. Regardless, it is true that small town folks love helping each other for no other purpose than to be of assistance."

Even if it gets you no closer to your financial goal for launch day, your local agencies and incubators may offer the educational or inspirational capital that you need in order to see this thing through.

CROWD SOURCING AND YOU!

By now everyone knows about crowd sourcing in one form or another – Kickstarter, Indiegogo, GoFundMe, etc. It is a proven way to test the market for interest in a new product, a film, an album, a cause. If enough people say "yes" to your project by giving you money, you get the funds necessary to bring it into the world as well as a captive audience who has already pledged its allegiance.

Crowd sourcing comes in other forms, too, though. Small-scale sourcing projects may provide that last bit of money needed for a piece of equipment, an expansion, or to get the lights turned back on. Again, from Calvin Friedrich:

"The concept works like this: if you wanted to open up your first coffee shop in Sikeston but were $10,000 short, you could try to sell 100 people $125 gift cards to your store for $100 each. This is a lot easier in places where you have a tightknit community and where buzz spreads easily. Also, if you offered this kind of unique idea in Sikeston, you are guaranteed to get free local press."

On an even smaller scale, crowd sourcing concepts can be used to keep small town trendsetters happy while everyone else catches up. I like to stay current in my industry. I also like to taste new or rare coffees and to keep my palette in check. In some cities, coffee professionals can sell ultra-special beans for $7 or more per cup or $40, $60, even $100 per pound. I buy very good beans at competitive prices, but there is a top tier of specialty coffee for which I have no market. Using crowd sourcing techniques, I could work around this conflict by assembling a handful of regulars who are always looking for something fresh and exciting. Together, we might commit to purchasing a few pounds of a small batch of upper echelon beans. In this way, I would be able to minimize my exposure, while keeping everyone happy. Plus, I'd get to try some amazing cups of coffee in the process!

B-CORPS AND YOU!

A recent evolution, Benefit Corporations, or B-Corps, obscure the line between profit-seeking business and social or environmental do-goodery. The classification has existed as a label or stamp of approval, sort of like Fair Trade or "free range," but some states now legally classify businesses in this manner. Restrictions may differ state-to-state, but the demand for positive impact in business is clear. Young people want to love brands who do more than make dollars, and many entrepreneurs feel led to their ventures by a desire to make the world better more than to turn a profit.

"There has been a trend in the past two decades of businesses having more than one mission," says Friendrich, again. "Although many economists find it easier to model business owners as 'economic agents' whose sole goal is profit maximization, it is not quite that simple. Rather, newer businesses – and particularly those who cater to Millennials – generally look to both create profit and be involved in some social purpose."

The B-Corps classification may be the answer for those following this trend. "By voluntarily meeting higher standards of transparency, accountability, and performance," those with B-Corps status seek to offer "a positive vision of a better way to do business."[3] If B joins S, LLC, Inc., and their friends nationwide, it could

[3] <Bcorporation.net>

mean tax incentives, grants, and other economic perks for doing business with a conscience.

SLOW GROWTH AND YOU!

Your plan could be flawless, but sometimes in small towns the money simply isn't available. Nowadays, you may not need to jump in 100% right away. Introducing your product or service online is in many ways easier than opening a brick-and-mortar location, especially in a small community. Creating the demand for your product while keeping the supply scarce could help you toward the day when you can do this full-time. There are countless examples of food trucks that grew into restaurants or freelance photographers who eventually required a studio space, but other types of businesses are now following this same path.

A friend of mine has a lifestyle product line and a vision for her brand to be stamped around every boutique from here to Timbuktu. Today, she has none of that – only a good design sense, a handful of products, and two hours each night when she gets home from her day job. Her plan is designed to take her from today to someday, fulfilling her career dreams without throwing her into debt, even if it takes twenty years.

First, she cultivates her brand image. She slaps her logo onto photos and pushes her message around blogs and social media. She talks to everyone she meets about her vision. The idea is to put her products into people's minds before it exists in their hands. When she gets us hooked, she gives away free samples.

Next, she will make sales. She has a series of pop-up shops scheduled around her town. Major retail brands and cutting-edge chefs have used the pop-up concept for a decade, but in small towns the idea is new and exciting. My friend will transform rented or borrowed spaces into a glimpse of her store for 24 hours at a time. There are some costs involved, but the price is far less than the overhead required when opening a full-fledged store with years on the lease. Even if sales are initially slim, the buzz generated by the events will send many customers to her online stores, where more frequent purchases are possible.

On it goes until she is ready to take the plunge. Hopefully, my friend's company will generate enough revenue online to pay for itself offline. Perhaps she will still need to borrow some money, but her company will show a record of growth, which will warrant the risk. Or maybe, through this process, my friend will discover that her local market is not ready for a product line like hers. Either way, this type of growth works well with her lifestyle and requires only the levels of time, energy, and money with which she is comfortable. For many entrepreneurs who want to avoid debt or retain equity, this may be a good option.

JUST YOU

However you fund your business, it all comes down to you. You may be fortunate enough to get your dreams financed by angels. You may win a pitch competition with a cash prize. You may have to empty your own pockets. Either way, don't be a fool. The burden is on you to take what little you start with and to turn it into your empire. Your employees trust you to pay them. The government demands its share. A lot rides on your financial shoulders now.

This may require you to sacrifice. If you default on promises to investors but continue to smoke a pack a day, no one has sympathy for you. The version of you who goes out every night, buys primo dog food, watches every minute of Netflix Original Content, or always has a fresh set of kicks might not be able to exist for a while. Someday, maybe, you could sail through life in the captain's chair and treat yourself to every whim and fancy. For now, you have to row the boat.

THE MILLION DOLLAR QUESTION

My friend and sometimes roommate, Ashley, is a creative person who is more into artistic endeavors and feelings than I am. She likes kitties. I like chess. At the time of this writing, she is about to launch a storytelling platform in the blog and social media world called *Dumb Beautiful Idiot*, and she is thinking very entrepreneurially about it. Using many of the same principles we've discussed in this book, she works through her brand daily, planning and budgeting and wearing all the masks. One day, someone might label her an actorpreneur. She calls herself a procrastipreneur.

Sometimes I subject her to the problem-solving drills that run through my head. While I cook or do laundry or unwind after work, I invariably ask myself questions that I think no one has ever asked and then try to solve them. Everyone does this, right? Wrong.

Me: "I wonder if we could increase crop yield by eliminating rows and pivot irrigation and instead use drones to spray, fertilize, and water the fields?"

Her: "…Ok."

The other day, for some reason, I began a discourse about her business and about being prepared for growth. I said something like, "…and I know this is probably obvious, but…" She stopped me short. Ashley reminded me that this weird dialogue in my brain is not normal, is not obvious, and should not be assumed in others. Entrepreneur nerds do it, but no one else does. She encouraged me to include these questions in this book.

So, here's one – the same one I asked her the other day. I've included space for you to fill in with your answers. Do at least three lines, and if you find this helpful, there are more questions and scenarios in the back of this book for you! Actually, they will be there even if you do not find this helpful, but that's how we talk. Anyways, here's the first one:

You've been in business for years when suddenly an investor calls. She offers you $1,000,000 if you can convince her that you know what to do with it. So, what would you do with it?

_____

_____

_____

_____

_____

_____

_____

_____

_____

_____

Even if you are not ready to expand on your own dime, you don't want to leave money on the table. An exercise like this prepares an entrepreneur to think about the next phase in his business. If that money showed up, he would be ready to put it to work. Likewise, and more likely, when the time comes to take out a new loan or to spend profits to grow the business, the entrepreneur who has this question answered will already have a plan.

PART III
PRACTICES OF SUCCESSFUL ENTREPRENEURS

FANDOM

BY BOB SCHOOLEY

People love The Ground-a-bout. They are loyal to a fault, and the reason is because it's theirs. Of course, I don't mean they "own" it in a financial sense. We're not running a co-op here. But it's theirs, nonetheless.

The town we're in (Jackson, MO) did not have a coffee shop when we started this journey, and their desire for one has been heard loud and clear. But filling an otherwise empty niche in our community is not the only (or even the biggest) reason we've been so fortunate in building a fan base. We sincerely believe in community spirit. As corny as that may sound, we believe in it at our core. We would go so far as to say that we don't believe that a small business can be efficiently built in a small community without that spirit being alive and well amongst the business startup, other business owners, the local government, and the public in that city or town. People, for the most part, live in or near a small town because somewhere inside them, they'd rather be involved with others around them at a much more intimate level than those that would choose an urban sprawl to cohabitate amongst the masses. Even if that means having to deal with some of the drawbacks of small town life, they want to feel like they are a part of something, anything, as opposed to being "lost in the shuffle," if you will. It's because of that yearning that scenarios like the show Cheers made for great television, where, at a local bar, they carved out a small, familiar corner for themselves in an otherwise huge, homogenized city. Come to a place where "everybody knows your name." That same scenario plays out daily in small towns everywhere at coffee shops, diners, mom and pop shops, hardware stores, etc. When you live so close to others and must share fewer places with them than others do in bigger cities, then you just learn them. In every way. Their names, their jobs, their families, their vehicles (Don't forget to wave while driving down the road. It's what we do here.) are all part of a beautiful tapestry, which is woven tightly over years of sharing the same spaces, cheering the same sports teams, and eating together at one of the six places to eat in town. Small communities make do with fewer offerings by their nature.

When one of our own decides to add something (a business) to the fabric of our community, we immediately take notice. When you open your doors, assuming you've done your job getting that word out to your market and assuming that you're offering something of value your market wants, they will come. If for no other reason than to see the new "digs" and to give you a shot to win them over, they will come. I've even found extra margin of error when it comes to pleasing my customers (though not infinite leeway, I assure you). Trust me when I tell you, they want you to succeed. Deeply. They know that new small businesses in their community are signs of great economic health. They've seen the fly-by-nights come and go and passed by empty buildings a million times over the years, especially in commercial historic districts. So, your success means more to them than you may think. Even more than they may think. It's also supremely important to other surrounding businesses. The more successful and complimentary businesses there are in an area, the more they all will reap the benefits of their numbers. We receive helping hands, expert advice, and favors galore from the businesses near us because they know (as we do now) that "all boats rise as the tide rises." It literally takes a village to cause a local economy to flourish, but lucky you...you'll have one if you play your cards correctly and follow all the advice in this book.

Here's where the most important part comes into play. Most people don't practice this, and some don't even understand what it means. I'm going to unveil this tip right now in a way that no one can misunderstand. It's total magic, unfailing, completely profound, and getting rarer by the day. You ready for the knowledge nugget I'm about to bestow upon you? Whenever they ask you what you're doing, or walk into your door, or call you on the telephone: BE KIND. I don't care how stupid or useless or tired you think that concept is, it is the most important advice I can give you. Even when you don't feel like it (which will be often), engage your customers. Engage your clients, engage your vendors, suppliers, and staff. Stop and converse with them. Learn what they're looking for, what they value, what they're missing. I cannot stress how far the effects of these actions will stretch across your life, in business and not. Learn people's names when you can. Clearly, we have more opportunity at this than most, because a first name is requested to write on your coffee cup, so we can call it out for the pickup, but I'm stunned every time I notice someone's face ACTUALLY light up with a smile, in shock, when I remember his name after only meeting him yesterday or a couple times last week. If you don't think that's a good start on building a loyal fan base, then you might as well stop reading, because there's nothing else I can say that will help you.

Additionally, make sure that you realize that what you are doing is, in fact, business. What I mean by that is, don't get so caught up in your own head, stuck on doing or selling things that may mean more to you than to anyone else, that you forget that you need the customer to purchase what you are offering. And where I'm going with that is, again, when it comes to decisions about your business going forward, ASK YOUR BASE. If you're adding or subtracting products, changing prices, picking a color for the walls, or whatever, ask your loyals. After all, they are who you're marketing to. If they didn't already feel invested, they will now. And it's not a false expression. They ARE now invested. They've helped build the place at some level. Even if their input on menu font was the only one they gave, they now "own" it. They're now a tiny figurative shareholder. I can't even count how many times my wife and I are working in our shop and those around us can hear us discussing decisions on how to move forward on a subject, so we just ask their opinions. If we're testing a new recipe, or deciding value-based pricing changes, or designing a seating layout, people (especially paying customers) have an opinion and feel very valued when asked for it. It may be a little unconventional these days, and of course, occasionally, you'll get a surprised response of "Oh, don't ask me!" But more often than not (by a landslide now) they will wade right off into our discussion with us, giving unedited opinions and experience that no amount of marketing money can provide. Now you have a qualified opinion about a product/price/choice from the person whose money will be spent on it. In essence, you've just made a future sale. Or 10. Or 100. They feel like an integral part of that tapestry we referenced earlier, and the feeling IS mutual. Next minute, we are ordering lunch for that day, so we might as well ask those sitting with us in the shop (because it's rude not to, right?). At first, most will decline, but after a while, they start to say yes. Now you've struck more than a business/customer relationship, and they are as committed as one can get. They feel like their money is extremely well spent when they see the owners on premises, every day, working as hard as the staff they employ. They can actually see where their money goes, as opposed to some corporate cloud where the effects of their money are so far removed that they'll never see it make a difference.

Allow me to illustrate some of those effects. On almost any given day, we have a rush between the hours of 7:00AM and 11:00AM. Now, as a coffee shop, we have customers that sprint in and bolt out to begin their work day. We also have those that have no place to be and who sit for many hours to sip coffee, eat pastries, or work on a laptop. Our group of "regulars" has grown enough now that there is usually one or more of them in the shop during all or part of that time each day. Not a single day goes by where I don't notice one of those highly-invested loyal regulars actually clearing the dishes off of the tables and walking to the dish sink with them or answering a fellow customer's question after they notice that we didn't hear it while busy making drinks or directing any particular operational issue as if they "own" the joint. I've witnessed regulars sign for packages, receive the mail from the postal worker, make innumerable amounts of drinks (for themselves or for others), wipe tables, dust, sweep, stock inventory, correct an overlooked issue, take on a support role for coffee roasting efforts, repair equipment, hang décor, water flowers (indoor and out), upsell others by positively talking about an item, and so much more. You think I'm joking or overstating it, don't you? I promise you I am not. That's exactly the sort of personal investment we're shooting for. You think those folks will be back, with friends, many times? You can bet your bottom dollar. Any day of the week, a newcomer would think that there are ten owners (or at least employees), when in reality, there is usually only one paid staff member on the clock at a time. We try to foster that sort of involvement by engaging the people on all sides of us and it has worked in Jackson, Missouri. It's not that we want the free help, it is that we want them to feel ownership. For these people, this is their shop. We wouldn't have it any other way, and we believe that they wouldn't either.

In summary, the business advice I think is the most effective, and certainly the most important, is a guideline you've been hearing since kindergarten: Follow the Golden Rule. Treat others as you'd like to be treated. It seems so simple, but if you really, really measure yourself and your business by this model, you cannot fail.

THE BACKSTORY

Bob and Serena showed up in my life sometime in 2016. Bob ran Uptown Jackson's very active economic development group. He owned a freshly remodeled building in the beautiful neighborhood, and a coffee shop was going to go in his building come heck or high water. My dad saw a story in the largest regional newspaper in which Bob said "any" coffee company should come open in his building. Obviously, the folks in Jackson didn't know about Parengo, yet. I aimed to change that before another coffee company got in my way.

Little did I know, Uptown Jackson prices property quite a bit higher than what Parengo was used to. So, after looking at Bob's very nice space, my dad and I hung our heads and casually mentioned, "Well, if you come across someone who wants to work closely with a local roaster and supplier, we'd be happy to train them. We'd love to see Parengo Coffee served in this town, but we can't afford it right now."

A few weeks later, after running the numbers and informally polling practically the entire town of 13,000 or so, Bob and Serena decided they'd just do it themselves.

Jackson wanted a coffee shop, and Bob is not one to pass up an opportunity.

So, we began. During our first training session back at my shop, Bob informed me that he did not care for fancy drinks and had a hard time believing that anyone in the world could honestly taste the difference between one coffee and another. We made pour overs. We French pressed and siphoned and pulled espresso. We talked about roasting and branding and steaming milk. At some point, the Schooleys told me how much traction their shop already had on Facebook, even though it had not opened. The Schooleys themselves, at that point, still did not know how to use any of their equipment, which they purchased on my recommendation alone, but the day was fast approaching when their entire shop's worth of machinery and inventory would arrive. It looked like Jackson would be a great town for a coffee shop and that Bob and Serena would be the perfect people to run it, if only we could teach them how to make coffee.

Within minutes of opening, The Ground-a-bout (a nod to an infamous round-a-bout nearby) had a line from the register to the door. A few months in, a video they made went viral, mostly from local activity. When my company, which I thought was well-established, gets 1,000 likes on an online post, The Ground-a-bout will get 3,000. Bob's phone rings twice a minute, and friends demand Serena's attention from open to close. Local craftspeople wait in line to display their merchandise on the Schooley's shelves, and friends volunteer time to sell coffee to other shops, to build marketing strategies, and to drive to other towns to pick up supplies. These days, as a group, the Schooleys and their regulars plan to expand throughout the region. They recently acquired my roaster, and, I'd like to proudly add, Bob can often taste the difference between one coffee and another now.

The Ground-a-bout does not just have customers, likes, and followers. It has fans, adoration, and devotees. It turns out, success as a small town entrepreneur cannot happen if one is only a good barista. One must also be a good person. Bob and Serena are known throughout Jackson, Missouri as being great people who own a coffee shop. And the line is still stretched to the door.

CHAPTER SIX

WORK

A while back, I attended a discussion series at Southeast Missouri State University. The speaker told interesting stories and gave his opinions on current events, but he really came alive when he answered a question about work ethic. Rather, the question was about success. His answer was about work ethic.

He got his career by buying a camera, teaching himself how to use it, flying to Somalia, and shooting his own stories on spec for whomever might buy them in the future. He made himself into a conflict-zone correspondent. When children grabbed his bags and stuck assault rifles in his face, he persuaded them to be his cameramen and bodyguards. Later, as a broadcast journalist in a studio setting, he arrived first every morning and stayed on set until everyone else went home. He worked tirelessly – chasing leads, fact checking, cold calling. Soon, the lead anchor on his show took a vacation, so this speaker asked if he could fill in. He performed well. The aging celebrity anchor who helmed the show valued his tee times more than his job, so over the next few weeks, the fill-in received more chances behind the desk. Eventually, the studio wondered why it paid the old man when the kid did all the work. The younger man took over the show full-time.

The speaker was Anderson Cooper, now the face, name, and personality of an entire brand of television. I've heard hundreds of Hard Work stories before, but what struck me about Anderson Cooper's was that he did not need to do it. He was born into money and privilege. He could have coasted, traveled in luxury, or pursued a half-baked passion project. Instead, he worked hard and put his life on the line to gain respect in his field in order to have a career that makes a difference in the world. That was his lesson that day: whatever you want to achieve, work harder than everyone else trying to get it. Rich or poor, that truth is the same. Even now, with a cornucopia of shows on multiple networks, he says he tries to be the hardest working person in the newsroom every day. He knows if he slacks, there will always be another Anderson Cooper ready to take his place.

In small town entrepreneurship, hard work can make up for much that you lack. Take your life seriously, take your town seriously, take your business seriously, and put every ounce of energy into them. You can't build an empire by talking about it. Get up and grab a shovel.

The small town entrepreneur knows how to work, but so do a lot of people. The difference is, one day the hard work could lead a small town entrepreneur to freedom from the daily grind, not to mention the satisfaction of sitting atop an empire. Here are four facets of work which every small town entrepreneur needs in her toolbox. One is a practice, one is a goal, one is a discipline, and one is a mindset. All are vital:

1) Go hard.
2) Be the best.
3) Know the most.
4) Fear comfort. Take comfort in fear.

GO HARD

I have had some terrible jobs, and I have flopped into bed at night already angry that I might accidentally wake up the next morning and have to it all again, but I had never so completely exhausted myself until I ran my own business. And it wasn't just one freak day. There were hundreds. In one day, I am barista, cashier, roaster, maintenance man, and custodian. I act as head of PR, HR, the CEO, and often OMG. In a week's time, I have gone from rewiring a Chinese roaster to rewiring an Italian espresso machine to rewiring the framed photo that fell off the wall. Expect 80 and 90 hour weeks for a long time. Heck, I'm not even the hardest working person in my neighborhood. Sam the Jeweler once closed down my shop with one final Americano to get him through a full night of ring repair. The next morning, he was my first customer. He hadn't been to bed yet.

Going hard is not just about breaking your back, though. Time and energy are not a magic recipe for success. They are tools commonly employed by those who succeed and commonly overlooked by those who do not.

Successful entrepreneurs make entrepreneurship a priority over almost everything else, at least for a chunk of time. If you're not willing to say "no" to fun things in order to build an empire and the future you want, quit right now. Go to work for someone else. A great life can come from a regular job. I can't stress enough how important this is. Unless you get lucky, this venture has to become your whole life for a while. Everything else must fit into it, be because of it, be for it, or fall away.

We live in a time when it is difficult to align actions today with goals for tomorrow. Would-be small town entrepreneurs often struggle with this. The other day at a leisurely dinner, a woman complained to me that people just did not support her business and so she did not make much money and was still trying to save for the slow season. Then she ordered another glass of wine.

Families in business who jump frantically from one thing to the next and beg for more time to get things done suddenly run off on spontaneous vacations. Once a guy begged me for a job. It was his dream to run his own coffee shop one day, so he wanted to learn everything he could from me. However, he only wanted to work an hour here or two hours there, he couldn't close, and please, don't ask him to come in too early. But he really wanted to work! Yeah right. None of these people have realized they need to go hard today in order to achieve their goals, even if that means sacrifice. And none of them run successful businesses.

On the other hand, there's my friend Clare, who used to own a business near me. Her business was known for three things: 1) creating gorgeous heirloom jewelry which was nearly indestructible, 2) maintaining a beautiful website which sold her pieces across the country, and 3) at one time operating the narrowest retail store in Missouri. Seriously, I think they had the record. It was like six feet wide. What no one ever saw was everything Clare did behind the scenes to make her success possible. She came in hours before the shop opened to set up new displays and to make custom bracelets by hand. She spent countless midnights in the light of her computer screen, balancing her books or updating online inventory. She stretched packing tape across thousands of boxes through the years to save pennies on labor.

Holidays stick out in Clare's mind as being particularly difficult in the early days. The season surrounding Thanksgiving and Christmas constitutes the biggest season of the year for retail stores. Retail business owners can't survive if they prioritize anything over their sales during that month and a half. Therefore, the Holiday Season for Clare meant driving to her family's gathering in rural Missouri, hugging everyone as fast as she could, eating a quick lunch, dropping off gifts, and speeding back to her store, where she'd spend all night preparing for Black Friday sales or post-Christmas exchanges and re-fittings. It was difficult every single year, and sometimes her family struggled to understand why she wouldn't just take one holiday off, but she made the sacrifices with future goals in mind. Three years ago, finally, Clare took off for a Valentine's Day - or she tried to. Instead, she ended up slammed at the shop all day, and customers lingered even after closing time. Just after 9pm, her date arrived at her store. They had planned to go out for dinner hours earlier. "I'm half asleep!" she protested. He smiled, cleared a space on the counter for the flowers and the hot meal he had brought, and began helping her clean up. It was the most romantic Valentine's date she could've imagined at the time.

Clare knew how to go hard. Events, special occasions, even relationships take a backseat for the true entrepreneur who cannot imagine failure. Luckily, sometimes, people are willing to go along on that ride with us.

BE THE BEST

For too long, small town folk settled for mediocrity. Now they demand the best. They've seen the best on TV, and they've tasted the best on vacation. When the highest quality is not available at your store, they do not mind driving to the next town over to find it. It is not in your best interest to merely harp on a "Shop Local" soapbox. Create a business that is not only one of the best in town but one of the best in the industry. Give other towns' folks a reason to drive to you.

My buddy Glenn is a photographer. He moves around a lot. One pitstop included a cool apartment overlooking the Mississippi River – big windows, high ceilings, original wood floors. This night, a mixed group of friends and acquaintances sat around his place listening to one of his hip-hop playlists and watching barges float by. When the mood is right, or when we've had too much coffee, Glenn gets fired up on certain subjects - photojournalism and hustling in particular. The mood that night was right on the money. He flipped through contact sheets from famous photoshoots and explained why the decisions made in each frame were important. He delivered a masterclass in why stories and the practice of telling them matter.

He impressed another friend who was new to our circles. "Wow, so like, what do you want to do with photography?" she asked. "Like, what's your goal?" After a cinematic pause, during which he gave himself permission to be honest, Glenn said, "I want to be the best."

Glenn wants to work for *The New York Times*. That's why he moves. He took a job at a small town daily paper, because every great *Times* photographer started at a small town daily. Glenn goes hard, often editing around the clock. On his days off, he shoots personal work or plays in his homemade darkroom. He's always pumping out new projects and applying new skills.

My friend goes hard every day because he has a clear career path he wants to walk down, but also because he wants to be the best there is. He knows that by setting greatness in his sights, his work will constantly improve, even at a small town daily. When a new camera comes out, he studies it like a med student studies for boards. If a photo blows him away, he figures out how the photographer took it. If staying up all night learning new software is required in order to be the best one day, that is what Glenn does.

If you provide a service, be the type who leaves clients feeling like they just worked with a pro. Become synonymous with "expert" in your customers' minds. Even though I've made thousands of lattes, I still analyze the appearance of every shot and try to get a little better with every pitcher of milk. I recently took a "Barista Basics" class just to make sure there's nothing that a beginner might learn that I don't already know. Whether it's on

Angieslist.com, Google reviews, or merely the word around town, rumors of your expertise will reach the ears of your clientele, and in a small town, reputation matters.

Lucky for you, being the best in a small town may not be too challenging. You might be the only one of your kind around. You might think this thing you do is "good enough." I hope you will not stop there. Remember, there is always someone coming right behind you, ready to take your spot. Be the best there is and work hard to stay that way.

KNOW THE MOST

I remember the moment it happened. I was a part-time cashier and 64-ounce Mt. Dew slinger at a small town restaurant/liquor/ice-cream/deli/barbecue/memorabilia/convenience store. This place was the classic way-it-has-always-been-done small business. There were no entrepreneurs around at the time. Between filling Styrofoam cups with sugarwater, replacing moldy ceiling tiles, and answering "I think we're out of that" a hundred times per day, I got scorched out. I began clocking out in my head long before my shift ended. One day, toward the end of my employment there, an older man tried to engage me in conversation. Who are the owners? Where are they from? What's in the chili? My eyes glazed over. Before I could stop myself, I blurted out those famous words. The man knew what I was about to say. He even finished the sentence with me, word-for-word. "I don't know. I just work here." As soon as it left my lips, I hated myself. The man shook his head and laughed at me. His eyes called me a piece of trash. I agreed. He never ate there again.

I remember that encounter, because even back then I knew I was wrong to treat a job that way. From then on, whether while roasting coffee or taking out the trash, I tried to become an authority on the task at hand. As an employer, I expect new hires to seek expertise at every level. On a typical first day at Parengo, employees learn how to ring up a drink, where we keep the dish soap, and how roasting affects green coffee's cellular structure. Within days, I expect them to know the difference between cold brew and our other brewing methods, at what temperature water boils, and how to answer the phone well. I never want a customer to know more about coffee than we do, but I also want us to be experts at the little things.

All the more pressure, then, for me to stay educated. Same goes for you, boss. One way to stay up on things is to read. Read everything. I devour magazines – *Barista, Roast, Fresh Cup* – as well as every book I can get my hands upon. Of course, the Internet is helpful, too. You could become an expert in anything these days just by watching videos online, so there's no excuse not to do it.

Good enough is not good enough. You may wonder, but why not? Maybe you could open a shoe store and do good enough to make a living and to have some freedom. Ah, but that is the mindset of the small business owner. Remember, it's OK to be a small business owner. I'm not trying to convert anyone. I'm only saying, there are people out there like me who cannot stop until they are Shoe Queen of North America. In order to get there, the Shoe Queen sold a lot of shoes. Thousands of people bought her shoes because they trusted her to sell them the best shoes at the best prices. They asked questions and got answers. If some of them had discovered that the Shoe Queen possessed only cursory knowledge of shoes, she would've never risen higher than Shoe Governess. Let your customers find themselves in your expert hands and watch them come back for life.

FEAR COMFORT.
TAKE COMFORT IN FEAR.

There is a spectrum with fear on one end and comfort on the other. We all operate somewhere on the continuum at all times. Often in the beginning, an entrepreneur is willing to give up a lot of comfort in order to live on the fear side of the field and to conquer it. On the flip side, the unwillingness to leave the comfort end of the spectrum is what keeps a lot of people from ever taking the first step toward their goals.

Alas, our tendencies slide toward comfort at all times. Eventually your daily duties are not as dire as they were when you first opened your business, and running your empire becomes routine. The weather gets nice and going for a bike ride or firing up the grill sounds too enticing to decline. Certainly, everyone needs breaks from time to time, and I am all for enjoying myself, but every practice observed one time too many can become a habit. Without realizing it, we slip toward the comfort end of the spectrum, and our businesses suffer. I would be willing to gamble that this slippage is easier in a small town, with cheaper mortgage payments and lifestyles keeping us comfortable.

For an entrepreneur, the fear of regret, of never having worked as hard as we knew we could've, of letting time and opportunities pass by – these fears are far more threatening than the fear of failure. Yet, failure looms near when one gets too comfortable. Building momentum takes minute after minute of hard work, but losing it happens before you even know it is gone. One day you are stuck running a small business just to survive and wondering what you could have achieved if you had remained diligent.

Far too many times I have given in to my immediate desires. I worked a long day. I'm so stressed out. I'll just rent a movie. I'll sleep another ten minutes. I'll worry about inventory tomorrow. I'll call him back next week. What could I have done with these hours instead?

It is easy to convince ourselves that we "deserve this" – a break, a night out, an extra tap of the snooze button.

However, those decisions add up, and the sum counts against our goals. It is much better to be uncomfortable now in exchange for avoiding our ultimate fears down the road. So, go hard even when it hurts. Put in the time to become the best at something. Take comfort in fear and fear comfort like a disease lest it consume your time and energy. Besides, the comforts you will be able to afford once your business booms will be way better than whatever you can scrape together today on a startup budget.

BALANCE
BY JAKOB PALLESEN

To paraphrase the wise words of the poet collective, Cypress Hill:

"Most people don't see how much work is really involved
In this startup life
I didn't know it
I didn't see it
I never saw it until I was actually in it
You really gotta be in it
To understand what it's like…

So, you want to be a startup superstar
And live large
A big house
Five cars
You're in charge.

Comin' up in the world
Don't trust nobody
Gotta look over your shoulder constantly."

Ok, maybe they weren't rapping about the struggles of being an entrepreneur, but it ain't really all that different. In this chapter, we're gonna get real real and down with the downs of the startup lifestyle. Now, that I got that out of my system, allow me to proceed.

We're not going to pretend that long-term entrepreneurial success doesn't come with significant upsides (why write this book if it wasn't an amazing journey worth taking?!). I get it, you want to be a big baller with loads of money in your bank account, a nice car, a bigger house than your neighbor, brother, and high school nemesis, maybe even some fame in your old hometown. Heck, if you're really successful, you'll end up on the cover of magazines with great sounding quotes you can't quite remember if or when you said. That may be the honest reality one day.

But the honest reality is also that so much hard work went into your success that you might already feel incredibly burned out. You're wearing down from working 70, 80, sometimes 100 hours, week after week. You made some money, but your family thinks the TV and microwave are doing more for them emotionally than you are. What are you doing, taking a vacation? Don't you know there's SEO to tweak? A stranger starts pestering you with emails, calls, and showing up on your doorstep asking you to invest in his trillion-dollar, innovative, disruptive tech concept that only he can pull off (oh, and he needs to outsource all the actual work to a low cost, foreign alternative, because, after all, he is the idea person, not the actual software developer). You're the local startup king! You get it! Share some of that wealth/time/energy/genius/connections with the next up-and-comer! There's always more to do!

All of your success and the legion of blood-leeching moments that come with it, can take a very real toll on your mental and physical wellbeing. Don't ignore that. You're doing more harm than good by soldiering through.

Time machine: You're 85, retired from the world of entrepreneurship, net worth is solid and plenty to pass on to kids and grandkids, and you should be nothing but satisfied with a life well lived. But you're not. No one really seems to remember or to care about all of this incredible business success you had 30 years ago. Kids and grandkids mostly refer to you as "Grandpa Money Bags," and strangely enough, there's some consistent seasonal trends in how often they pick up the phone to call and say hi (Good news, Christmas is getting closer, so that phone should start ringing anytime now). You finally read that old, dusty book about living a meaningful life that someone gave you when you were 25. It's not hard to put the puzzle pieces together and see that perhaps the incessant focus on your business only created so much meaning in your life, but maybe, just maybe, wasn't the only thing that should have been meaningful.

If you haven't already done this, go to Google and search for something like "biggest regrets at the end of life". What is in the top 5 of almost every single list? You got it: "I worked too much and didn't spend enough time with family and friends." In all fairness, these lists almost always also include the challenge of not having saved enough for retirement (With your massive entrepreneurial success, that, of course, won't be a problem, but just in case the bank account hasn't surpassed the million-dollar mark, this is also a pretty significant issue to consider on your entrepreneurial journey). Still, the point is: many successful people regret the excess time they spent on work instead of seeking a balance of work and non-work life.

Ok, but the solutions don't have to be complicated. You can work your tail off and still find some real balance. Get home and eat dinner with your family, spend time with them, and turn your phone off when you're with them. If possible, bring your kids with you to work sometimes, so they'll understand what you do all day. Foster a culture in your company that respects (heck, maybe even encourages) everyone's need to have some equilibrium between work and family/friends. And not to get too crazy, but have you considered occasionally taking a small vacation with your closest people?

But there's more. Yes, this is the hippie-dippie, feel-good vibes section of the book where we also tell you to meditate on a regular basis. No, seriously! Learn how to relax your overhyped brain as a way to stay mentally fresh and alert. It's not just to make sure your family and friends continue to like you, but it's also good for the bottom line of your business. Think about it. If you're stretching yourself thin day after day, week after week, month after month, you won't be able to make smart and clear decisions. You'll make those stupid mistakes that will cost you a lot more money than you'd be willing to admit to anyone.

"I'll relax when I'm rich," you might be thinking. How rich, though? At what point will you feel comfortable enough with your income to actually take care of yourself? According to a recent study, it appears that only so much money will actually contribute to your overall happiness, anyways. The latest numbers indicate that once you've passed the $60-75K per year income level, more money won't do much to make you happier.[4] That's for an individual, so throw some dollars on top if you have family to support, but the point remains the same; mo' money ≠ mo' happiness.

[4] Amy Patterson Neubert, "Money Only Buys Happiness for a Certain Amount," 2018, Purdue University News, 20 Aug. 2018 <https://www.purdue.edu/newsroom/releases/2018/Q1/money-only-buys-happiness-for-a-certain-amount.html>.

Regardless of how accurate the research is behind these kinds of claims, they do appear strikingly obvious and intuitive once you look at them. It might seem like common sense - the kind of common sense that apparently isn't all that common when you look at how many people spend all their time in their 20s, 30s, and 40s working to the bone and then wishing they hadn't later. We can learn from those who came before us.

This is all about valuing your mental and physical health as part of your long-term strategy to avoid complete burnout at a critical moment. Passion and grit will take you a long way but having some tools in your pocket to help balance the hardest moments will keep the boat floating a lot longer. Beyond some regular meditation (which doesn't have to be more than 15 minutes a few days a week), there are many other ways to stay mentally and physically healthy. The list is really quite long, but of course no one can do all of it. Find a few things that work for you. These should not be confused with bad excuses to binge watch Netflix instead of working on growing your business. So, if you find yourself putting "3 hours of daily Netflix" on your list as a "mental health" break, try again, and find something that actually adds value to keeping your body and mind fresh, clear, and ready to roll.

Below is a list of suggestions. Borrow from it or make your own. Remember, we are entrepreneurs because we envision a world we want to build – take some time to live in it along the way.

Suggested ways to make more money by not burning out:

- Write down your vision and reason for being an entrepreneur. Know why you choose to sacrifice other things in life – carry this with you. Update as needed. Take it out and remind yourself occasionally.

- Respect your sleep schedule and get the amount you need (not saying this will be easy, but it's doable) - and no one is impressed if you claim you only need 4 hours a night. Our biology tells us we need 7 to 9, and you're not so unique that you can cut 3 hours off of that without consequences.

- Define success to yourself in your own terms and focus on clearly defined priorities that make sense to your life. Write it down. Update your definition of success as needed.

- Have a few very close, trusted family or friends that you can ask to "keep an eye on you" so they can let you know if you start looking overburdened. You might not want to listen to them right away when they bring this up, but you'll likely realize if they're right.

- Include your family into your business (not by

giving them ownership shares but by bringing them to work and letting them see what it's all about).

- Jog or cycle to work.
- Do yoga, Pilates, or other trendy exercises.
- Eat really healthy foods a few days a week.
- Find a good mentor with whom you can talk openly about tough challenges.
- Spend time outdoors in nature.
- Write down things that make you happy or for which you're grateful every few days.
- Give back to your community.
- Donate money. Donate time. Mentor someone yourself and give her or him your undivided attention.
- Read and learn about time management, decision making, life balance, and happiness.
- Go visit a professional mental therapist.
- Find a mix of physical and mental exercise that works for you. Maybe you do pushups between calls and play chess with a friend every Saturday morning. Maybe you mow your own yard. Maybe you take a walk every evening with your grandmother and listen to good stories.
- Get a little dirt underneath your fingernails every now and then.

ABOUT THE AUTHOR

Jakob Pallesen is recognized for his trademark daily three-piece black suit and clear-framed glasses, but he is known for being an invaluable resource to startups in Southeast Missouri. As the Director of the Small Business & Technology Development Center at Southeast Missouri State University, Jakob coaches, teaches, inspires, and encourages droves of entrepreneurs, students, and colleagues each year. I've found his data, formulas, contacts, book and podcast recommendations, and time infinitely helpful and enjoyable.

Jakob hosts a regular Facebook Live broadcast in Cape Girardeau, Missouri in which he speaks to local entrepreneurs about all kinds of subjects. He is currently producing and hosting a podcast called "In Search of Success," which asks entrepreneurs about success in life and in business, real happiness, and – you guessed it – the balance of it all. Subscribe to it wherever you get your podcasts.

CHAPTER SEVEN

THREE MASKS

Masks are used throughout literature and film to illustrate dichotomies or dualities. In *The Mask*, Jim Carrey plays the nice guy who wants the woman who loves bad guys. When he adorns an enchanted mask, he becomes a cartoonish and supernatural Don Juan who robs banks and dances a mean Rumba. In some iterations of another story, Bruce Wayne pretends to be a rich playboy whom the world loves to hate, and he wears a mask to become a ruthless hero whom they hate to love. The drama mask symbols themselves remind us that all stories are either comedies or tragedies. The world of masks is mostly binary.

However, a successful small town entrepreneur will have to learn how to simultaneously and constantly wear three masks. That's right, three! These three masks represent ways of thinking or mindsets. They are not mutually exclusive, thankfully, and there is a lot of overlap, but they may require slightly different sequences of synapses firing around your brain. Lots of people are well-suited for one mindset or another. Your survival requires all three.

The Three Masks of Small Town Entrepreneurship (3MSTE, if you're following along) are these:

1) The Tycoon

2) The Brewer

3) The Architect

Each allows you to transform into a key piece of the puzzle you need to become in order to keep your company healthy and ever moving forward. Wear them all at the same time or change into each one at least once a day. It may get sweaty in there, but weekends are what showers are for, am I right?

THE TYCOON

A century ago, Henry Ford and others like him took entrepreneurial thinking to a new level. We have cars in Detroit, so let's make people want them in Detroit. What if we can make the people in Ann Arbor want them, too? Well, let's find a way to get the cars to Ann Arbor. Wouldn't it be cheaper per car if we sent 100 at a time, each sharing a piece of the cost of transportation on a freight car? It sure would, so let's send 100. Well, what if we could produce 100 cars per hour? What if we could do that 24 hours per day and in a dozen cities? And so on. Ford championed mass production, which works in the producer's favor only when enough units are sold to outweigh the costs of production and transportation. An entrepreneur wearing a Tycoon Mask must maintain one steadfast goal: more.

My dad is one of the greatest salesmen ever to walk the earth. Over the past 50 years, he developed a reputation for being one of the go-to guys when a company wants to assemble a farm equipment sales team. He sells combines, headers, tractors, sprayers, pickers, drills, dirt buckets, and whatever else a Midwestern farmer might need. My dad is among that old school group of guys who never took a math class above multiplication and division but who can spout off the answers to long questions about financing and interest rates before I can even get my phone out of my pocket to click on the Calculator app. He understands how to build trust with clients, how to get them good deals, and how to take a "No" in stride.

His number one rule is simple: keep selling. He rarely stops to calculate how much commission a vendor owes him or how many units he still needs to move this month in order to make his house payment. He knows those numbers and can pull them out of nowhere when asked, but his focus every day is on more. A 6% cut of X units may be good, but a 6% cut of X+1 is better. When it comes to sales, my dad wears a Tycoon Mask.

In a previous illustration, we met an executive at Three Bear, LLC. named Mr. Pappa. For our purposes in that section, Pappa was kind of a rube. However, if porridge really did go gangbusters, Mr. Pappa would be vindicated. His aim at more, more, more, if successful, would eventually shoot his department past its break-even point and would then yield a profit. Pappa might be a Tycoon.

The Tycoon Mask will keep you focused on one necessary goal. You should be selling. You should be selling more. You should attempt to sell more every day. There are other considerations and priorities, but in order to keep this company around for a while, you have to think like a Tycoon.

More.

More.

More.

Thinking like a Tycoon works in a small town entrepreneur's favor in more ways than in simply maintaining focus. If your small town is anything like mine, then its citizens love chains. I mean franchises, big brands, Super Bowl commercials and all. They're from somewhere else, so their glossy menu boards legitimize our choices, but they still serve chicken fingers and sides of ranch with everything, so there's no reason to worry that we might be forced to try something new. My town has an old, established fried chicken joint with the greatest biscuit sandwich known to man. This past summer a chicken chain opened up with that cute cookie cutter country vibe. Police had to regulate traffic as cars lined up to the highway. Even with a time-tested local chicken place, the locals freaked out over the chain.

Within a year-and-a-half of opening Parengo, I made some good progress. Still, many in my town held back their loyalty. Two cafes - that's nice. In a few stores - yeah, we've heard of that. We've been meaning to check that out. Roasting for several other companies – oh, that's real, real good. On the news, in the papers, trophies on the shelves – cool, man.

Then, our region's one and only high-end grocery store finally said yes. My friend Kara and I had been pursuing this store for months. After a dozen changes to our bags and weeks spent figuring out how to purchase bar codes, we got the deal done. Suddenly, everyone I met was a huge Parengo fan. By wearing a Tycoon Mask and constantly pursuing deal after deal, attempting to put one extra bag of beans on every shelf that would let me, I suddenly seemed like I had achieved franchise-level status for Parengo. That fancy store legitimized our brand in the eyes of our small town market. Every leg of every revenue stream increased immediately. Soon after that, a man came in for the very first time and told me he loved Parengo. I'm in the shop every day, and I had never seen him. "It started here, you know," he told me, as if I didn't know. "We've always gone, since it opened. Just went to one in Cincinnati, too." Sure you did, sir.

THE BREWER

Take off your Tycoon Mask for a second and try on The Brewer. The Tycoon is a crazed loner, obsessed with more, but The Brewer is a more practical mask, down to earth. The Brewer thinks about details – clocking in, taking inventory, perfecting recipes and pricing every ounce, pour, and scoop. It involves minding costs, cutting expenses, and obsessing over pennies, which add up substantially over thousands or millions of units. Paper cups costs money, so I make a rule that employees must use ceramic mugs when on the clock. I notice we are dumping a little bit of milk down the drain after every latte, so I adjust my pours to save just that much. The bank account is idling, so I send staff home early. The trash bags we use smell nice, but they cost more than the unscented kind, so we switch them. The Brewer minds the details.

Like every white guy with a beard, I tried my hand at homebrewing a couple of years ago. Just like coffee roasting, beermaking requires a science-like approach. Specialized equipment is required, like brew bags, carboys, bottle filler siphons, and racking canes, and all of it must be sanitized to prevent even the tiniest foreign particle from entering the process and screwing up the entire 5-week long saga. The names of the main phases sound like Slytherin House students – Wort, Mash, and Fermentation – yet, it is imperative that the brew maintains precise temperatures at each stage. Heat, chill, oxygen, and even stray dust could kill the yeast who make the magic inside and could cost thousands in product down the drain.

Brewing demands attention to detail such as the Brewer Mask allows, but every entrepreneur can benefit from this skillset when it comes to sales, especially in a small town. Jim Koch believed he should not have to go through the rest of his life and drink a bad beer ever again. With attention to detail, quality ingredients, care in the process, he knew our regular American beer could be exceptional, and he assumed enough people in the country would be able to tell a difference between good and bad beer to make his detail-oriented pursuit profitable. Samuel Adams Boston Lager introduced much of our country to craft beer before it was cool, and Koch, now a billionaire, still tastes several batches per day for quality control (and for fun).

During the early days of Parengo, I knew my small town market might resist my prices. I imported beans, roasted each batch myself, tasted my product constantly, hand-poured one cup at a time, and steamed milk with nearly a decade of practice, but at the end of the day… it's just a cup of coffee to some people. I suspected we would need to double down on the details part of things. Perhaps our confidence and expertise would convey the message that this was no ordinary cup of coffee.

My first baristas – Katie, Amy, Maddie, Annie, and Theda – and I developed our *mise en place*. We dusted and wiped down the machines constantly. No stray splatter of milk could even dry before we swooped it up with a quick finger. We practiced latte art with our faces practically in the mugs. As a visual cue to our quality and mastery, I displayed our coffee brewers like trophies along the wall – a French press, a siphon on a red beam heater, a flannel drip pot, a Kalita Wave – and I let customers see us weighing doses of beans down to the gram. We made every drink with precision. This was no ruse. We actually knew what we were doing, and we did it extremely well. However, the display of our craft and the constant concern we took with every detail of every cup provided our early adopters with a sense of value that is now indecipherable from our brand. Wearing the Brewer Mask taught me common sensical tasks, like counting pennies (also an indispensable detail), but additionally, it allowed me to add quality that transcended "just a regular cup of coffee".

THE ARCHITECT

In my early teens, I played a lot of management games – Sim City, Roller Coaster Tycoon, even Harvest Moon. I loved the way I could build wild attractions while manipulating the smallest details to run a superefficient staff or infrastructure. I also loved naming cows. These games allowed me to zoom out to see the big picture. I could see where a Ferris wheel would look best or how far my power plant was from my fancy residential neighborhood. They also allowed me to zoom in to find out if my customers were enjoying themselves and if my tax revenue would be enough to pay for my roads and if my heifers needed milking.

I spend a lot of my time considering the big picture of Parengo and its place in the world. Is my neighborhood an attractive destination for my target market? What elements in the zeitgeist may contribute to demands for new frappe flavors? Do visitors to our website get the sense that we are the company I want us to be? I read Jim Collin's *Good to Great* and began wondering how each barista, past and present, fit a role in my company and how I could hire better fits for the team. I read *Make Your Mark* by 99U and was inspired to develop a theory that Parengo filled a missing version of home role in the community, which meant our coffee was only an excuse for customers to get what they really needed.

I may only arrive at clever or valuable insights 1% of the time, and the time spent on the big picture does not immediately pay off in literal dollars, but keeping one's ship on its theoretical course is ultimately one of the most valuable roles of the entrepreneur. Some of your partners and peers may function with a mindset that is more like a small business owner's. They will roll their eyes at your highfalutin conceptualizations. Ignore them. When you find a concept that helps you realize a new level to which your company could aspire, flesh it out. Frank Lloyd Wright ignored his haters, too.

Architects are creative, but I hesitate to call them artists. The title "Artist" sounds diminutive to me. It evokes travelling on one's parents' money and couch surfing with fashionable friends in lieu of the chains of signing a lease and making it to appointments on time. Creativity may be one of my favorite traits in a person, but one cannot convince me of his creativity by calling himself an Artist or a Creative. Let the work do the talking.

If you've ever walked into a well-designed building, you knew it instantly. The way the elongated shapes of the windows, curtains, and columns drew your eyes to the ceiling to make you think the office's height was great; the cast of the light in angles tilted across the floor at a certain time of day to give a lobby an endless length; even a door that closed perfectly behind you – these signal that a master of the craft conquered the math and fact of what exists already and imagined them into what could be. Architects know materials and load limits and bedrock, but they can also see where the sun will set, how to angle each room for its optimal view, and how a breeze could stir in a courtyard.

Frank Lloyd Wright is probably the greatest contributor to American architecture. He looked at the plains, fields, pastures, and woods in towns like yours and mine, and he saw the creatures who inhabited the space. He noticed the strong prairie winds and the violent storms, the bugs and humidity and snow. In Wright's time, people cleared trees and built houses straight up and down in the Victorian style, pointing at the sky. These houses may be pretty, and they might be sturdily built, but they make no sense on the horizon. Much of the American landscape is flat or rolling with small hills and relatively low trees, and he envisioned domiciles for the human animal to contribute to the scene without destroying or interrupting it. Wright's homes are lines and right angles, planes of rooms and decks and landscaping, as if grown there within the forests and streams. When you see one, you just get it.

The Architect Mask urges the small town entrepreneur to envision a world that is better because of her trade. She then takes that vision and applies it to her company, asking the biggest questions. Where are we going? What need do we fill? What product or service could I dream up next? The Architect Mask cannot be adorned by someone who is merely creative with no skills. You, small town entrepreneur, are an expert, though. You know your company inside and out. If anyone can see the unseen sunset and angle us all so that we can feel its glow on our faces, it is you. Take us somewhere incredible.

THREE MASKS AT ONCE

Viewing your company through three masks helps you to know your company with intimacy and to work tirelessly for its success. The Tycoon gives you momentum, the Brewer reduces friction, and the Architect gives you trajectory, letting your company soar where you point it. When a small town entrepreneur can live in all three masks simultaneously, she is like a master conductor directing woodwinds, brass, percussion, and strings in harmony. Well-thought out brands are the results of this symphony.

CHAPTER EIGHT

COLLABORATION

Picture me, gesturing wildly with my hands like I do, lots of pointing and pounding my fist into my palm. Before me sit seven unfortunate twentysomethings who happened to walk into a small town coffee shop on the wrong day. Maybe they seemed hip or artsy or said something about "getting involved downtown." Whatever the reason, I asked them to join the crew of my latest project to bring people to the neighborhood – Tributary Film Festival.

I designed Tributary to become a yearly event during the summer months when business slows and before most other festivals in the area gear up. I thought maybe Downtown Sikeston could become an unlikely movie lovers' destination for one weekend a year. I planned for my crew and I to go find movies made in the Midwest, to turn Downtown businesses into theaters, to make and sell merchandise, and to get donated all the money and supplies it would take. I thought it'd be huge! Everyone in the state would want to come! We might find the next Brad Pitt! At our first team meeting, I unloaded this whole scheme onto my volunteers.

"Now, are there any questions?" They stared back at me through a tension I couldn't name.

"What's a film festival?" one finally asked.

So, I did most of the work myself. My dad popped popcorn for the audiences, and my mom sewed together the mobile movie screen, and some friends participated in making short films to show or running social media for the event, but by-and-large, I tried to do it all alone. Tributary lasted two years. The filmmakers were very kind to me and generous with their time, but hardly anyone came. It mostly sucked.

Now picture me at the espresso machine making gourmet hot chocolates. My sister and brother-in-law decorate plates of *petit fours* with chocolate drizzle in the back of the room, while two of my nieces light Sterno cans and show customers how to assemble our "Tableside S'mores" special. It's Valentine's Day. My parents burn marshmallows in the corner on their own little Parengo date, and customers pack in all night long while the *Ukes of Hazard,* a local duo, pluck romantic ukulele tunes in the background.

The event was my sister's idea, and I met it with "Yes, that sounds great, but I'm going to need help." My whole family decided to make a night out of it. Everyone pitched in, from shopping to advertising to baking, and we nailed it.

My friends make fun of me sometimes, saying that instead of being born as a single human, I should have arrived as a committee in order to accomplish all of my goals and ideas. While it's impossible to be born as a committee (I assume. I'm not a doctor.), I do wonder what it would be like to work in those storybook wonderlands of team-culture like Google or Phil Jackson's Chicago Bulls. Small town entrepreneurship is far from that.

While a small town entrepreneur needs to be a jack-of-all-trades, she also must learn to collaborate. All of Parengo's greatest achievements are the results of collaboration. More accurately, our success is a bulleted list of me begging friends to help me or taking a friend's advice, such as the time my friend Lance told me to write a chapter about collaboration.

Friends made my logo, designed my flyers, ran the company's Facebook and Instagram accounts, built our websites, and recorded our radio spots. Friends took our photos time and again and made our television commercials and silly YouTube videos. Friends came to my events, showed up early to set up and stayed late to clean. Glenn, Mallory, Ashton, Gracie, Mark, Derek, Lance, Maddie, Annie, Camille, Jay, Ashley, Julie, Michelle, Matt, Alex, Jake – these people don't even answer my calls anymore without anticipating "Hey, could you do something for me real' quick?" Although I get all the credit, without them and so many other people pitching in to decorate, move things, taste things, click "Like", or add a song to our Spotify playlist, Parengo would be just me ladling coffee out of a tub in the trunk of my car. No one wants that. It took a village.

Other collaborations of the business-to-business variety strengthened our network and helped fill in gaps in our product lines and service. We traded coffee for pastries with Sweet Mayhem, served other goodies from The Knead and Cravings, and partnered in events with Cup 'n' Cork, bread + butter, and Piper's, all area cafés. We donated gift cards or beans to every fundraiser in town. We set up coffee bars at the annual Chamber of Commerce Banquet in exchange for tickets to the event. Ember & Valor, a local men's product manufacturer, put our coffee in their beard oil and our beans made it into stouts and porters at local breweries Minglewood, Buckner's, and Saxony Hills. Each partnership introduced my products to their customers, presented their products to my customers, and doubled all the advertising we could do for each event by doing it together.

Beyond the obvious, an attitude of collaboration is healthy because it gets you involved in your community. Your community is your market, aka, your customers. Therefore, to be involved in your community is to be more intimate with your customers. In a small town, you are not only in a business-customer relationship – you're also neighbors, members of the same organizations, members of the same gym, and friends with the same guy. Your survival depends on your willingness to collaborate with your patrons.

When it even appears to be in the realm of reasonable, I say "yes." When the Chamber of Commerce wants to host a Young Professionals mixer in my shop, I stay open late. When a group of misfits wants to host a Doctor Who 50th Anniversary party, I stay open late and decorate my front door like the Tardis. When Coffee with a Cop, a Republican gubernatorial candidate, or the local chapter of Democrats want to use my shop for an event, I stay open late and keep an open mind.

Two customers of mine, let's call them Annabelle and Clarence, vibrate on one end of the spectrum, while I… well, I don't even vibrate. We could not be more different. To say they are dog people does not quite paint the full picture. That'd be like saying Prince Charles is "into" royalty. The only animals who live in my house are in the refrigerator, while I imagine Annabelle and Clarence's dogs allow them to have their own human-room in the basement when they're good. They use terms like "fur babies." I use terms like "my rugs are spotless."

Annabelle and Clarence brought me a gift years ago. I don't even remember what it was. Something to do with coffee. It was awesome. I was flattered. Then they brought some origami. Annabelle is maybe the most gifted paper folder I've ever met. Her stuff is mindboggling. We put it up on a shelf as decoration. Then one day, they asked us to keep Dixie cups around so that their dogs could order "Woofesso" when they came in. They provided the cups and said they'd pay for every shot of whip cream to fill them.

With a miniscule amount of participation, Parengo gained a couple of fans. Annabelle and Clarence found a place to belong, to believe in. They felt like they contributed to the essence of the place. They were part of our team. And in the years since, no one has been a bigger advertisement for Parengo, nor has anyone spent more money. Annabelle picks up four or five drinks a day to take to coworkers or friends. She fills up two or three loyalty cards each week and gives them away whenever she meets someone who hasn't been to our shop. We owe her a great deal of gratitude.

Your abilities to usher people from customers to fans to friends is so much more important than your product or service. It requires letting the real you show, listening, and saying "yes," and it is a kind of collaboration between your vision for yourself and their vision for you. That's scary, I know. But the reward is a town full of people who know you, who cheer for you, and who have your back no matter what. Everyone wants to be on the winning team. So, be a team player.

PASSION, OR SOMETHING LIKE IT

The generations currently entering into or rising within the workforce are the first who were told "You can be anything you want to be." With everything as an option, it is nearly impossible to pick one attractive future to commit to for life. As a result, many of us are rapidly approaching middle age and still wondering what we should do with our lives. Here's the thing about passion: you don't need it!

Someone said to me recently, "It must be so nice doing what you love every day. When did you know you wanted to do this?" It took me a moment to understand what she was talking about. Doing what I love? Did she mean coffee? I like it. I love to drink it. But is this supposed to be my passion or something? I started doing this because I saw an opportunity – a need that I could fill. I keep doing it because it is lucrative. Whether or not I am "supposed to" spend my life making coffee is a different story.

As an entrepreneur, anything can look like your passion for a while, and you should treat your ventures as if you could not imagine living without them. Starting, growing, inventing, dreaming, problem solving – the entrepreneurial life is what we are attracted to. That is our true passion, whatever form it takes. When we come to terms with that, we can stop waiting around for that one special dream path to open up before us, and we can start getting stuff done.

So, if you're an entrepreneur, get up off the couch, dream up a killer idea that fills a need, and get to work. Wait for Fate to whisper in your ear, and you might be waiting forever. Instead, go hard. Learn everything about something. Try to be the best at it and keep trying even when everyone around you takes a break. Be uncomfortable for a few years, and passionately build an empire that may or may not involve your passion. Your hard work can't pay off until you put it in.

CHAPTER NINE

THE ADVICE CHAPTER

You planned, you thought through everything, you became an expert and worked hard, you created a brand, raised a startup fund, and now you're reading the end of Part III, hoping I will finally offer some practical steps to success. Here's the rub: the rest is common sense. You now have the tools in your toolbox to succeed. As long as you show up every day and go hard, you have as good of a chance as anyone else.

The remaining chapters of this book require The Architect Mask. If a small town entrepreneur contacted me today and said he launches his business tomorrow and only has time to read 50 pages of my book, I would tell him to read Part IV. It's mandatory. But before we become Architects, here are a few simple pieces of advice from my realm of experience. You can keep The Brewer Mask on for these.

COCKTAILS AND FAJITAS

Some of my local watering holes are very fine, dependable establishments. I can count on that vaguely chlorinated odor, as if they are breweries or hotel lobbies. The cushions in the chairs are perfectly worn-in. My order is familiar. I know at least one person who will walk in the door.

When I travel, I like to try out fancy bars that go a step further, though. That one step makes a huge difference. These places are part laboratory, part greenhouse, part museum, and part apothecary. At the end of the bar, the shakers and swizzle sticks wait next to an herb garden – every garnish sprouting fresh beneath a grow light. Tinctures and house-made bitters in various jars and bottles line a shelf. Ice comes out of machines and molds, all shapes and sizes, each for a different purpose. Charred rosemary and smoke from who knows what gets trapped beneath my glass like a spider at a picnic. The bartender (even if his curly mustache makes my eyes roll) delivers a swift crack to a handful of cubes with the back of a bar spoon. It's the most satisfying clunk I've ever heard. I hand-crack ice at home now when I need to calm down.

If my bill comes out ten dollars higher than what I am used to at home, I hardly seem to notice. Now, I realize many people are not interested in this. They just want a beer at a dive and the simplicity of it all. However, the lesson of the mixologist is that details matter. Little things can take something fine and make it exquisite.

In another realm, consider the American fajita. Marc Leible, one of the entrepreneurs behind Delta Document Shredding in my town, brought this to my attention. The steak has to be good. It absolutely can't be bad. People are here for the sustenance of a meal. But they're paying for the sizzle. The sizzle is not real. Tex-mex restaurants and steakhouses everywhere plate your meat on the skillet and squirt it with oil, water, or citrus juice to make the sizzle happen. Sometimes the skillet is rigged up on an induction heater. However they create the sizzle, the steak was cooked just like any other steak. Even so, without the sizzle there would be riots in the streets.

Before I even owned an espresso machine, I paid a talented graphic designer named Jason Courtney to create the Parengo Coffee logo and bag design. We went back and forth for weeks distilling the gibberish in my head that would become my brand's story. Jason came up with a template that looked approachable yet fancy at the same time – a small town business that takes itself seriously and puts out a luxury product with as little pretentiousness as possible. Jason nailed it.

Next, I found a digital coffee bag printer, Roastar. com, and began the back-and-forth again, choosing size, gussets, valves, foil or craft, matte or glossy, tin ties or zippers. When it was all said and done, I panicked for a moment. I had just spent more than $2000 on digital artwork and coffee bags, but I owned no coffee beans to put in them!

Parengo's story required the professional design and packaging because we sold a product which our market viewed as ordinary. After all, some diners give coffee away for free. The burden fell on us to convince our neighbors that they should stop and consider how an ordinary thing could be made with care and could then become extraordinary – and could cost fourteen dollars for 340 grams. When they walked into our shop for the first time, they said, "Wow!" When they looked to the retail shelf and saw our quality packaging, they said, "Wow some more!" When I offered a smile and a conversation about the beans, why we do things the way we do, how we roasted these very beans right back there in that contraption, right here in their town, and then showed them how a pour over works to make an amazing cup or capped their mochas with a neat rosetta, they became fans. Cheap coffee could not cut it once they held a superior product in their hands and felt its sizzle.

Like mixologists and fajita pros, you serve clients something they could get elsewhere. The way you do it – the sizzle, the conviction, the kindness, the tirelessness – is the reason they pay you instead of someone else. This is even more true with your service. Your timeliness, your attitude, and your honesty create waves. Every detail you dial in sets you apart. You planned, you became an expert, and now you have to execute every single day down to the minutiae. Your smile, your handshake, your ability to stop and listen instead of plowing ahead – these details become your reputation in your small town. Remember, word spreads quickly. In no time, your sizzle will be the talk of the town.

This is some of the most basic yet most valuable advice I can give. It blows my mind how many small businesses neglect the sizzle, yet it is so obvious once pointed out. I've hammered it home again and again throughout these pages, but that is because I believe it is one of the primary features that separates a small town entrepreneur from a small business owner: a small town entrepreneur figures out his brand story and executes every detail.

CONSISTENCY

From almost every single small town entrepreneur I ask, the one piece of advice that comes up consistently is consistency. Your products and services must hit your high mark every time, but I think this principle is even larger than uniformity. Certainly, don't let the quality of your products fluctuate. However, the reason entrepreneurs I've interviewed are successful is that they are dependable. They are consistent in everything they say and do. In a small town, leaders are relied upon to attend events, to be on time, never to miss a payment. They make promises, and people expect their word to be their bond. They admit when they made mistakes and work to correct them. Consistency is the one-word answer that underlies a successful way of life here. It's a good one to live by.

Southeast Missouri's climate is what would happen if an insane nine-year-old played SimCity and hated all of his citizens. Instead of four seasons, we get to enjoy 175 microseasons, which last maybe a day or maybe ten at a time. People here are used to driving in harsh conditions, but at least once a year something wicked comes our way, and the town gets frozen into an ice cube overnight. It's like living inside a snow globe.

If you were to stop shaking the snow globe long enough for the chaos to settle, you'd look deep inside and see my little shop on its little street. There would be my dad and me, our vehicles parked willy-nilly in the snow. I'd be shoveling, and he'd be spreading salt on the ice beneath the sludge – all in an attempt to be ready when 7 AM arrives. If one regular customer decides to brave the conditions and get her coffee at her normal time, I want to be open.

Year-after-year of this, with rain and snow and ice and broken air-conditioners and power surges blowing breakers, there will be days when I cannot see the worth. I might spend a lot of money on a part or run frantically to catch all the leaks in the ceiling, and then so few people come through that I lose money. However, after five years of it, I received a great complement from Mike Marshall, our Economic Development Director. At a session of our small business incubator, he told the group of fresh entrepreneurs that Parengo Coffee stood as a great example of consistency. That was nice to hear. People were paying attention the whole time.

I notice a lot of small businesses, especially restaurants, try to do too much. What could work as Colby's Burger Shack quickly becomes Colby's Burgers, Chili, Hot Fudge, Candied Yams, Fortune Telling, and Katana Sharpening Taqueria Emporium (Now Serving Biscuits & Gravy!). The era of "The Customer is Always Right" culminated in ten-page menus, ensuring every single customer could find something he or she could palette. But customers are wiser now! We know there's a whole world out there we have yet to try. You're the expert of a little slice of it. That's why we come to you. You tell us what is good.

The only consistency you achieve when you offer a little bit of everything is consistent mediocrity. Plus, you will run into logistical problems. We ran out of yams because we needed the fridge space for the milk for the gravy. As a quick solution, we tried to candy some potatoes, but we had to throw them all out, and now we can't make fries to go with the burgers, which is the only awesome thing on this epic manuscript of a menu anyways! Instead of being consistently great at one thing, Colby's becomes a consistent nightmare to patronize and to manage.

Focus on consistency. Menus, product lines, services, and bonus features can grow over time. Master each one and consider the value your company adds to the conversation with every additional piece you offer. Give people the same level of amazing every time, on time, and in time.

A SENSE OF HUMOR

People are funny. I am (obviously by now) an advocate of taking ourselves seriously in order to elevate our companies and our towns, but at the foundation of it all, we are just people, and we do funny things. People sneeze, violently and to the surprise of everyone in the room, right in the middle of a sentence, and they make that face like "Where did that come from?!" That cracks me up. People accidentally flatulate at work. I die laughing every time. We spill things and break stuff and mess up our sentences without rhyme or reason.

Taking myself seriously leads to long, arduous years of doing the exact same things every day with no sick days and few vacations all in the hope of success at the end of it. However, powering through those long, arduous years would be impossible without a sense of humor. You will have hard times and even harder times, and you will not see your empire unless you persevere.

While moving Parengo from its original location to its current home, I spent days as a barista, afternoons painting walls and digging 40-year-old carpet glue off of linoleum, then coupled back to the original shop at night to roast for several hours just to survive the next day. Hovering over the hot drum, watching beans spin around a cooling tray over and over again until well past midnight, I would catch myself calling out color commentary like the roast cycle was a horse race. Sometimes I'd feel inspiration and work out stand-up comedy routines about baristas and hipsters, basically making fun of myself to myself. I wrote an entire meditation guide, mostly tongue-in-cheek, called *The Coffee Tao* based on becoming one with the grinder, the steam wand, or the drip. I either went a little crazy, or else I'm hilarious.

Sometimes I think I might expire if I have to make one more frappe, going through the rigmarole of small talk for the millionth time. Then, when I least expect it, something comes along to make me laugh. Recently, a lady stormed toward my point-of-sale for the first time. She seemed angry.

"I hate coffee," she opened.

"Oh. Well," I replied. "We have smoothi-." She cut me off.

"Nope. I need coffee. I woke up craving it, and I'm mad as heck about it. I have five kids, and I never once had a craving any time I was pregnant, but every time one of my brothers gets someone pregnant, I crave chocolate. I don't like chocolate, either. This time, I woke up craving coffee, which means I need to call around and find out who's pregnant and chew somebody out."

See, that's just funny. None of my hard work, expertise, marketing schemes, or efforts toward building up my neighborhood brought her into my shop. The only reason she would ever walk in would be if the universe played a cruel trick on her and switched up her strange cravings. That day, it happened, and I giggled to myself as I suggested she order a mocha just to be on the safe side. The next frappe I made didn't seem so boring. A sense of humor will keep you going."

OTHER PEOPLE CHIMING IN

Just in case I missed something, I asked my friends to pipe up. Several entrepreneurs in Southeast Missouri have small town success stories, and I wondered what their tips would be to someone considering small town entrepreneurship. I half-expected to hear too specific, almost unusable advice such as, "Never roll pennies for a deposit on Fridays." Or "Don't forget to turn your OPEN sign on early in the Winter on a South-facing street." Instead, I received a bunch of fantastic replies. These people know what they're doing. They take their companies and their clients seriously and put a lot of thought and love into their practices.

Here are some of their responses. Many talked about going the extra mile and consistency, which we already covered, but much of the rest of my friends' advice was unique. I am so proud to be working in a small town near people like this:

Mackenzie Price, *Shelter Insurance* proudly in Sikeston, MO

"Most importantly, I have always made it a priority that my client feels comfortable and at home in my 'office'. That they know they are always welcome to bring their children, dogs, and stories. At the end of the day, sometimes all a person really needs is to talk and for someone to listen. I don't want the first time they need to call me or come see me to be on one of the worst days of their lives, aka, the death of a loved one, house fire, tornado or car accident." She also reminds herself daily to handle rejection with an attitude of reflection and a mind open to learning from each experience. Mackenzie is a steadfast volunteer in our community and a ubiquitous smiling face at ribbon cuttings, mixers, festivals, and any occasion held to celebrate someone's success.

Carissa Stark, *Mary Jane Burgers & Brew, Jackson Street BrewCo*, revolutionizing Perryville, MO

"Create a culture that you are passionate about for your team and your guests and your community, and live by that culture every day. Have high standards and hold your team accountable to uphold those high standards. Be genuine, be hospitable, and be compassionate EVERY DAY." Carissa and her team invested in a small downtown neighborhood and sparked a movement. Even with only about 8,500 people living there, Perryville is now one of the coolest nightlife spots in our area, and Mary Jane is opening another location in nearby Cape Girardeau soon. Everyone around here talks about Carissa – always positively – and wonders what she'll be up to next.

Laurie Everett, *Annie Laurie's Antiques, The Indie House*, the human cornerstone of Downtown Cape Girardeau, MO

Years ago, I looked for expansion opportunities in Cape Girardeau, and everyone with whom I spoke said the same thing, "You have to talk to Laurie." She is always growing, learning, renovating, and adding the coolest new ideas to her businesses. She is a huge part of the growth of Downtown Cape and a constant cheerleader and volunteer. Also, she and her husband, Rocky, are two of the nicest people I've ever met. Here are three things that are important to Laurie's daily practice:

1) "I always take advantage of opportunities because you never know where that path will lead. What may start as a person selling one item could lead to an entire estate."

2) "I ask a lot of questions."

3) "I'm a morning person. Some days I get more done before 10 AM than some people do all day."

Lynn Lancaster, founder *Jay's Fried Chicken, Rochester's Delicatessen, Sweetgum Gallery, The Art Spirit*, owner *The Inside Story*, Director of *Historic Downtown Sikeston*, innovating while preserving

"You have to have a quality product, you have to have great service, and you have to document everything. And you have to know your product. I knew how much a tater tot cost. I knew how much an order of okra cost. I knew how many pieces were in each bag. Total knowledge of every product." Lynn has opened, managed, or purchased more businesses than the rest of us combined, no matter who you are. During his time at the helm of Downtown Sikeston, the neighborhood has gained more momentum than at any time in the past 40 years.

Joe Recker, *State Farm Insurance*, *Midtown Storage*, working hard in Sikeston, MO

"I was taught by an older mentor: 'successful people do the things unsuccessful people aren't willing to do.'" Joe started his agency at the age of 23 with no clients and no salary. A lot of people would not be willing to do that, but now Joe is a recognizable and respected presence in our business community.

Michael Haugh, *Bootheel CrossFit* shaping up Sikeston, MO

"Fake it 'til you make it." Michael remembers a terrible day when he ran into someone at a grocery store. The lady was so happy to see him that it turned his whole attitude around. He realized that he could do the same thing for his clients. He now makes an effort, no matter how he feels that day, to greet people when they walk into his gym, to hold conversation, to try to turn their days around. He also learned early on, during a stint in sales, to ask questions and then shut up and listen to the answers. "I would lead the conversations where I wanted them to go, and I wasn't getting anywhere." Listening can lead to sales, but it can also make you a better person. He and his wife Courtney are the joyful, laid back nucleus of the local fitness community.

Anthony Cervantes, *Ember & Valor*, looking good and feeling good in Cape Girardeau, MO

Tony and Lance built a product line, brand, and reputation on elbow grease and values which have stood the test of time. Their efforts are aimed along the lines of that adage, "The biggest mistake a small business can make is to think like a small business." Here are fourteen other tips Tony works by, in no particular order:

1) Quality > Quantity

2) Customers are smart. You can have great packaging and advertising, but if you don't have a great product,

you'll fail. You can spray paint a rock with gold colored paint, but at the end of the day, it's just a rock.

3) Know how much you did in sales last year, and set a goal for where you want to be this year.

4) Know how much is in your bank account. Check at least once a week.

5) Know who your biggest competition is and watch what they do, good and bad.

6) Use file storage software such as Google Drive to organize receipts, legal documents, design work, notes, social media items, etc.

7) Utilize social media for advertising.

8) Make friends with other business owners.

9) Bank with a local bank and develop a relationship.

10) Utilize a line of credit account with your bank.

11) Look at sales growth in percentage, not just in the dollar amount.

12) If you buy t-shirts for giveaways, get quality materials. Don't just give them to anybody. Give to people within your target market. They are walking ads. You want them to wear it, otherwise it'll be used as a shop rag or yardwork t-shirt.

13) Get a small notebook.

14) Use an accountant. They give peace of mind, they save time, and they assist with different business stages.

Emilie Stephens, *Annie-Em's at Home,* the jewel of Cape Girardeau, MO

"When it comes to finances, always have some small amount of cushion to fall back on. You never know when you're going to have to fix a water leak or have a snowstorm that forces you to close for a few days. It makes things way less stressful if you have something put back for those more difficult times. Also, to completely contradict what I just said, don't be afraid to spend money. Sometimes you have to take a leap of faith and invest in something when it's your slow time of year or when you don't think you need to be spending the money. For example, for years I wanted an awning for my storefront, but I put it off because they're so expensive. Two years ago, I worked up the nerve to buy the awning, and it's been amazing to see how much more traffic and how much more I get noticed because of it. Basically— I spent money, but it's now making me money."

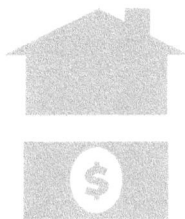

PART IV
BRANDING: YOUR BUSINESS & YOUR TOWN

CHAPTER TEN

TELL A STORY

More than a product or a service, you are founding a brand when you set out to build an empire. You are selling an experience. You could be the best of all time in your field, but with a crappy brand, you will not thrive. Likewise, plenty of subpar products sell billions of units because they are a part of a cohesive and compelling brand. Your company's brand should be the first and last story you tell every single day, especially as a small town entrepreneur.

Vision, Mission Statement, Motto, Core Values – the corporate world is not full of HR and PR buzzwords because they love making posters. No, big businesses understand that every aspect of their companies add up to tell the comprehensive stories of their brands, and they use these labels to break down the elements of storytelling. The difference between success and failure can be the difference between telling a good story and telling a bad one.

If brand stories are dramas, then the most recognizable ones are like major motion pictures, with producers overseeing every detail, a credit reel a mile long, and every actor ready to perform at Oscar level. Wal-Mart is a Summer blockbuster. Target is a Spring comedy you didn't expect to be so good. Shake Shack is on the festival circuit at the moment, and In-and-Out is a cool series on cable. Calvin Klein has one show on Broadway and another on a national tour.

Far too often, small town businesses settle for being community theater. Roles are double- and triple-cast, costumes are pilfered from moth ball attics, hair and makeup are abandoned to chance and a deep red blush. A microphone is inevitably glitchy, and each scene contains one forgotten cue, but the crowd keeps coming back because the kids are cute. The mistakes are forgiven. No one seems to mind.

Small town entrepreneurs cannot accept "no one seems to mind." That may be good enough for a small business owner, but for us, the play is not adequate unless it could stand up next to the greatest shows in the world, even if we choose to debut it in a small town. Yet even with our determination to succeed and expertise in our fields, many of us are stumped when our businesses fizzle out.

Brands are built by asking questions and making decisions. Questions one should ask before even deciding on a business name include Who are we? Who are our customers? Where do we make our money? What value do we add to our customers? Decisions made when answering these questions compile to form your vision. How you carry out that vision – every choice from your wall decor to your on-hold music – form your brand story.

Two stories: Heather and Jim. Heather cut hair, and like many in her field, she possessed entrepreneurial tendencies. She loved being her own boss, setting her own hours, and engaging clients with new technologies at the time – text messaging and social media. Heather texted appointment reminders and ran specials on Facebook before anyone else thought to use these media in her small town. Heather went to church with a young man who attended a nearby seminary. The school enforced a century-old rule which required male students to keep their hair high and tight. Heather charged the young man only five dollars to line him up once a month, called it a "student discount," and told him to spread the word around campus. Soon, Heather trimmed and washed the scalps of dozens of young clergymen in training. They each told other friends, and Heather became popular. She stood on the verge of running a great business.

It didn't last long. Heather was what a few years later our culture would label "a hot mess." The best barbershop chairs in the world are therapeutic, but unique to Heather's chair was a reverse confessional feature. Perhaps it was the aura of all the future priests passing through the chair each week, but instead of becoming a good listener, over time, Heather grew more cantankerous. She spilled her guts endlessly, her clients trapped beneath her clippers, forced to listen to her woes – raising a teenage daughter, finding a good man, could've and would've and should've. Heather was clearly unhappy, and every week her dramas unfolded with new and worsening degrees of anguish. Eventually, Heather began arriving to appointments later and later each week. Clients planned to wait between five to forty-five minutes and braced themselves for rollercoasters of emotional chit chat. This became Heather's brand story. It didn't take long for her customers to find less stressful ways to get a haircut.

Jim made the best sandwiches in town. He told everyone so, and a few of his close friends vouched for him. He knew exactly how to smoke a chicken, and his proprietary sauces were family reunion staples. After years of talk, Jim's wife finally heard enough. "Alright," she said. "If you're such hot stuff, then why don't you open up a restaurant?" Jim wasn't one to back down from a challenge.

As a professional chef, Jim's motto was simple, "Let the food do the talking." Sign a lease, dust the place up a bit, and get down to a man's work of putting meat on bread. His OPEN sign pulsed its blinky neon heartbeat for five whole months. Good sandwiches were not good enough.

Heather and Jim never considered the stories their brands told. Or maybe they never considered their brand at all. Heather would have responded to this issue by saying, "I just don't have time to think about that stuff right now! I'm running around like a chicken with its head cut off!" Jim's take would be, "I don't tell stories. I just make sandwiches. Did someone say chicken?" Even by neglecting to tell their brand stories, Heather and Jim were telling their stories. Heather's brand clearly said, "I offer thrown-together, whenever I have time, cheap haircuts for students, and my life is a spiraling rocket of chaos!" Jim's brand told a different story every day: "I don't care about myself enough to take this seriously, and you aren't important enough to eat off of a clean table."

When we talk about branding, we are not merely talking about logos. I use the term "brand story" to remind myself of how all-encompassing a brand really is. Every ad, every flyer, every Instagram post says something about a business. Even *not* advertising and *not* posting to social media adds to a brand's story (probably not in a good way). But where does one begin?

SIGN TOWN – A MISGUIDED APPROACH

A group of city leaders in a small town - Sign Town - held a meeting to discuss new and improved signage around town. They wanted everyone involved in the decisions from the CVB to the Chamber to the Public Works crews who would install the signs. The meeting was packed with every entity who wanted any kind of say in what the town's signs should look like, where they should be posted, and to what they should direct traffic. They spent hours on size, shape, materials, reflective or non-reflective, the optimal locations for arrows, what gets its own sign and what doesn't. It was nearly lunch before someone thought to ask, "Why do we need new signs? What do we want them to accomplish?"

Sign Town needed new signs. It's true. But the outdated signage was only a symptom. Over the previous few years, the town underwent a noticeable change. New businesses were popping up and landlords were renovating. Local leadership felt this change and knew they needed to step up into their roles in this fresh environment, but they failed to diagnose Sign Town's true location on the path of change. Instead of beginning with new signage, someone should have thought to begin with big picture questions. *Who are we? What do we do best? Where do we lack? Whom do we want to attract? What story are we trying to tell?* Colors, fonts, logos, shapes and sizes can only be decided once the big picture is clear.

Suppose, for an example, that a town is famous for its yearly Spring Carnival. This event brings in families from all over the region for one night only. Recently, the town's growth came in direct proportion to its hospital's growth. A whole new subdivision of large homes sprang up because of the influx of upper-middle class residents who quickly raised the per capita income of the town. The town's research suggests that the new segment of the population increased the perceived quality of life in the town, but the new families do not care for the Spring Carnival. Even though those who have been around for a long time adore the Carnival, they also hope to continue to grow their town, and they hope to continue to attract higher-income professionals like these new additions. So, in thinking about *Who are we?* or *What story are we trying to tell?* this town might want to focus its branding on its great medical community and year-round quality of life features rather than on the one-night-a-year event that does not contribute to its new growth.

A small group of creative folks in Sign Town came up with a package of ideas for how their town could rebrand, but no one in charge could agree on what this town wanted to be. Should it be branded as a great place to live? The creative group presented a cool way to get that idea across. Was it a town full of innovation and small businesses? The group drew up a brand story involving imagery from the age of Edison and Tesla. Was it a Southern town? An ag-centric town? A town rich with history? The answers to each of these questions could take the town's story in a dozen different directions. Eventually, when these questions are well and answered, only then can we talk about signs.

BEGINNING

Every good story has a beginning, a middle, and an end, and the best storytellers know how to escort their audiences on a journey through these stages. The journey has to begin somewhere though, and the beginning of your brand story will require the most time, energy, money, and care. You only get one first impression, as the saying goes, so you have to nail this part.

The first 20 minutes of every movie are my favorite part. Honestly, I would enjoy movies more, on the whole, if I only watched the first 20 minutes of every movie. This part of a screenplay is usually called The Set-up. It's where the really great storytellers reel us in. When all the explosions begin pounding away and the bullets whizz by and the cars turn into alien robots, I fall asleep; but in those first 20 minutes when we meet characters for the first time, when their traits are revealed in subtle hints like wardrobe and how they treat their moms, when we are introduced to whole worlds of wonder and magic – give me that stuff all day.

Treat each customer's first encounter with your company like the Set-up. What do they see when they look you up online? How is your company introduced to them when they pull into the parking lot? If they call on the phone, email, or walk in the door, how are they greeted and welcomed? What do they first hear and smell? With every color, texture, temperature, and tone, you can set up your audience to receive your fully imagined experience.

MIDDLE

The middle of your brand story probably consists of the part that made you want to go into business in the first place. Before you were an entrepreneur, maybe you were simply a good cook, a good salesperson, a good host, a good carpenter, a good caretaker. Eventually, you decided to go into business doing this thing. Now, you go hard at it, you are the best at it, you know the most about it. Even so, mind the middle.

How you present your products and services should never become commonplace. Your customers' experiences doing actual transactions throughout their whole lives as your customers should live up to the story you want your brand to tell. The middle is the part they will tell others about. You hook them with the beginning, but they will recommend "that place with the cute sweaters" to their friends. This is the easiest part of the story to commit to autopilot. That makes it the easiest part on which to slack.

Turn out great products every time. You are the expert, so never act like less than that. Make spending money with you easy and enjoyable. Consider where customers stand and sit and wait and congregate. What is it like to use your website's Live Chat feature? How do the forks feel in their hands?

We talk about "line of sight" at my shop. We have a lot of stainless-steel surfaces and to us they always look clean. We wipe them down constantly. If I walk around to the other side of the counter though, the light reflects differently, and I can see all kinds of gunk and smudge. I worry that I tell the story of an inferior brand when I am unaware of my customers' experiences. Now, when I say, "line of sight," employees know to look for smudges from every angle.

With our drinks, we want consistency of texture, flavor, viscosity, volume, and color. We want latte art on every latte and whipped cream never to touch the inside of the dome lid. We want to offer straws to each customer and to put the spout on the lid opposite the cup's seam to prevent leakage. All of these tiny things seem insubstantial in themselves, so it's easy to neglect one or two as the day goes by. However, no matter how great our Set-up was, if we allow ourselves to forget the little parts of the Middle, our story becomes very lame very quickly. The Middle requires diligence and perseverance through the repetition.

END

If you want to get a group of TV nerds arguing, mention the final episode of some beloved series. Opinions will be strong. "*Seinfeld* was inconsistent. *Bob Newhart* threw it all away. *Mad Men* – say what? *Lost* made me want to die. *Dexter* made me wish I'd never been born." The ending is hard to get right.

How many times have you left a movie theater furious that you just wasted two hours? Yet, I bet the same is true for you at the theater as for the TV nerds on the futon at home. A bad ending overshadows hours or years of brilliant storytelling. An hour and a half of your movie-going experience was probably great. That last little bit ruined it for you and ruined your whole night as a result.

Conventional wisdom offers plenty of advice on this subject. End on a good note. Finish strong. Leave them wanting more. We could also draw plenty of analogies. The audience in a jazz club expects each song to resolve. The best restaurants understand the art of the dessert. The most exciting events in sports are walk-off homeruns, buzzer beaters, and sudden death shootouts.

Anticipate how customers will feel when they leave you. How will they follow up? Make it easy for them to buy more, to comment, to share, and to find you again. Even if you do not serve dessert, there has to be some way for you to end on a good note. It costs nothing to help an elderly patron to her car out front or to say "thank you" or to shake hands. Our Parengo Coffee Club shipments go to customers who may never set foot inside our café, but each includes a sticker or a handwritten postcard. I realize people could easily spend their money and time elsewhere, and I work hard to gain the public's attention, to carry my story through their experiences with my company, so on my best days, I want them to end their time in my shop feeling noticed and appreciated.

Easy, right? So, imagine you put in a lot of hard work to craft a beautiful logo, menu, café experience, and service staff. Your food came out perfectly. Customers were transported from the moment they walked through your doorway. When they're all done, they ask to meet the owner to pay their respects. Instead of tying this story up nicely, you ask them to hurry up and leave and throw them your middle finger. That ruins the whole story! Likewise, a customer may have a great experience and leave satisfied, but he will never forget the way he drove around the neighborhood six times because your address is listed incorrectly on your goofy website. Think about what your audience is receiving every step of the way, and you'll be on the right track to telling them something they will want to hear again.

CHAPTER ELEVEN

PARENGO'S STORY

Owning businesses teaches us that we are not as smart as we think we are. Before opening, I developed a hearty concept of what Parengo's brand would be. Little did I know that, in a small town, people quickly let you know, in a thousand subtle ways, what story they want you to tell instead.

KODAWARI

You see white smoke pouring out of a small chimney behind the building as you pull up. You discern the source of the smoke as soon as you open the door. The tiny roaster hums and whirs in the back of the small, narrow room, and the whole place smells like toasted nuts. The cypress barn wood walls hold the aroma by now, baked in over a thousand batches. Indie rock greets you as you figure it all out – but the "we built this guitar with our own hands" kind; more White Stripes than Peter Bjorn & John. Walls are brick and cement, and the floor is stained concrete, with the pattern of the ancient original tile glue still visible. Butcher blocks act as countertops, and homemade light fixtures and chalk board signage round out the look to keep it from edging too far toward "country-chic."

There's me running between roasting, which I think I must do in order to make money, and training a barista on the minutiae of her Chemex technique, which I think more accurately tells our story. "Just a smidge too quickly. And too wide. Look, your pour should be the circumference of a half dollar. We want to be perfect every time."

My first blend, and one of the only ones we ever put together, I named Kodawari Blend. To me, it evoked a tableau of martial arts masters and sushi chefs. Kodawari is a Japanese concept, a sincerity of effort and focus on the journey toward perfection, knowing one can never reach that end. Parengo displayed coffee as a craft. I wanted us to picture ourselves as sensei of coffee with kodawari infecting our every action. We were scientists practicing the disciplines required to perfect our art. Coffee brewing equipment adorned the long shelf down the wall and looked like beakers and flasks and graduated cylinders. We engaged customers in conversations about countries of origin, the differences in brewing methods, and the molecular makeup of milk.

A few early adopters loved our approach. They'd visited shops like ours in St. Louis or Chicago, and they were ecstatic that our small town now had a coffee lover's oasis just like the big cities. Fairly quickly, however, we saturated that market. Everyone who was going to get down with our kodawari was already down with it.

After a few months of self-doubt and racking my brain, I realized something crucial. Lots of people came into our shop just to see what it looked like. They didn't care for coffee, but they had stories about Red's Bar, which used to occupy our building, or about the Malone Theater, which used to stand in the lot next door. They wanted to see the old brick and what we had done to the place. Once they got inside, they grew curious about our barn wood cabinets and trim, which came out of a now-defunct restaurant that locals loved for decades called Fisherman's Net. We refurbished it and turned it into a hip feature to accent our artisanal approach to coffee, but the majority of people who popped in were more interested in telling me their memories of the seafood joint where the wood used to be or about the barn they grew up playing in than about how we made the lavender syrup.

After developing some familiarity, returning customers eventually ventured to the back of my shop, where I ran the roaster. They'd see me loading batches – or more often than not, covered in grease trying to fix the thing after a short blew fire out the backside like a rocket – and they'd ask questions. We spent more time discussing the fire or the machinery or my tools for filling and sealing bags than we did talking about coffee.

The concept of kodawari as a touchstone of our brand story was not wrong, but it was only a piece of the puzzle. This is the middle of America. Things carry value – land and brick, metal and wood, boilers and gears and wheels. The stories of things that make up our work outlast the humans who used them. Collectors fill this town. Saturday morning yard sales brim with pickers before dawn. It took me a while to get over myself, but eventually, I admitted it: the La Marzocco, a heavy aluminum and steel hunk of beautiful Italian craftsmanship that pops and pumps until cascading espresso oozes out of its mouths, would bring in more customers than my knowledge of coffee growing altitudes and almond milk ever could.

To our customers in our small town, our value was in our all-American, D.I.Y. way. They loved the way we hand-crafted every drink with sincere kodawari intention, but they equally loved the way our pitcher rinser was installed flush with our countertop. Smell the smoke from the roaster as the beans pour out, see a businessowner wrenching at a stubborn broken grinder burr, and hold a bag of Parengo Coffee in your hands, made right here in Sikeston where Red's Bar used to be. Know its quality from its weight and the work you saw go into it. That was the story I should have told from the beginning.

HOME

It's a Saturday morning in Southeast Missouri. Even at 6:45, the air sticks your shirt to your sides and breathing takes effort. Some type of winged insect launches itself twelve inches at a time, and hundreds of its buddies follow suit every time you step through the grass, whose dull barbs seem to slap at your ankles for disturbing its slumber. No itch or discomfort can thwart you today, though. You're a competitor.

The Second Annual Parengo Coffee Great American Summer Corn Hole Tournament begins in an hour. Your team, Corn Thugs 'n' Hominy, faces off against Legal Minds, a husband-lawyer and wife-therapist combo, in the first round. Your opponents are already throwing practice bags and wearing their matching shirts, made just for the occasion. You and your partner still need to warm up. Underhand tossing bean bags toward a hole fifteen yards away tires out the shoulder, especially when you could wind up squaring off against Corn Casserhole or the Old Corny Fellas, who are favored to win the championship again this year.

The Parengo staff whips in and out of their building next to the grassy playing field. They mix up cold brew cocktails for the day and set out jugs of water. Theda uncovers chips and dips and buns and condiments on a patio table, while Larry flips burgers on the grill behind the coffee shop. Their children and grandchildren and several other duos of regular coffee drinkers park on the street and unload lawn chairs. The pair who wins today's corn hole tournament wins a cash prize and Parengo t-shirts, but everyone gets to enjoy the day. It should be a great one.

Sometime around our Second Annual Corn Hole day, I realized our brand concept needed tweaking. During our first three years, we wore off our novelty. The new car smell was gone. Business grew every year, and loyalty stayed at an encouraging high, but we lost that impressiveness quality. People expected three-year-old Parengo to be a part of their routine as if it had always been so. This is not a problem, but a loss of definition and awareness could lead an entrepreneur down all sorts of dark paths. I wanted to make sure we kept a handle on our identity so that we could always be figuring out where we were going.

About this same time, I began drawing up plans for our new location. Our wholesale roasting business picked up every year, and two or three new shops sprang up in our region all at once. So, I bought a new roaster – bigger, shinier, more efficient. When it arrived, I would be able to get a whole day's worth of roasting done in under an hour. My capacity would increase tenfold. However, the new machine would not fit in our original building. Seriously, it wouldn't even make it through the door.

Right across the way, beyond two streets and a small park, a bookstore wanted to sell out, building and all. Before I knew it, there I was moving shelves and picking out flooring. The 1915, two-story former home of Woolworth's would house my new roaster and updated coffee shop perfectly. And, since we'd be moving locations and renovating the old building anyways, the timing seemed right for reconceptualizing my brand.

Who were we now? What primary function did we serve? Did our customers choose us for our coffee or for some other need we filled for them? Could we continue to grow and to stay motivated if "craftsman" or "D.I.Y." defined us? Would quality staff for years to come be able to latch onto those categories like the earliest ones did?

That Summer day, while playing corn hole and eating potato salad, I found the answer to a lot of these questions. Our customers feel a sense of home in our couches and chairs. Larry and Theda are the parents. The baristas are like siblings with whom you share your hopes and dreams. Open Mic Nights bring the electric feel of a sleepover on a Friday night, and these corn hole tournaments are like cooking out in the backyard with a neighborhood full of friends and family. We eat our breakfast together before you head off to school, or you collapse into our big, comfy couch after a long day at work to chill for a few minutes and to listen to our music.

I designed our new shop with the concept of *Parengo as Home* at the forefront. The bar is the kitchen, so it's brightly lit, adorned with green to represent herbs and produce, and covered in white subway tile to inspire feelings of a shiny kitchen wall or floor. The pastry case is glass like refrigerator shelves, and stools pony up to the counter like an island or a breakfast nook. Fluffy couches and chairs surround coffee tables with rugs underneath. A lamp and a chandelier bring the lighting lower in the room in those areas, casting a living room glow over the scene. In the back, the roaster stands on a slick, grey epoxy floor with large double doors behind it and a workbench filled with tools nearby, representing any home's garage.

Our marketing messages follow suit. We encourage and speak with familiar language, sort of like a family might embolden and joke around with each other. Instead of only showing the prettiest pours and the most perfectly staged backdrops, we show mess from time to time. Our Instagram feed resembles what you might text to your sister rather than an average corporate display. This might all sound like amateur psychology, but 2018 is our most profitable year yet.

VISION

Some of the most brilliant entrepreneurs in history casted visions and then stuck to them. People laughed at them, called them stupid, wrote them hate mail, or liqui-dated their backer funds. Still, in the face of seemingly ev-eryone yelling at them to stop, these men and women per-sisted. They owned their Optimism Bias to the extreme.

Adam Sandler's pockets are wicked deep, and he made some comedy classics, starred on SNL, and pro-vided dozens of catch phrases for my friend group when we were in Junior High. The dude is comedy royalty. It seems like he was destined for greatness. However, he tells a story about the early days when he was a no-name stand-up comedian begging to go on stage at every open mic night in Los Angeles. Every now and then he'd get on, all of nineteen years old and the weirdest person the audience had ever seen. He'd do characters with their unrealistic voices, and he'd play guitar and sing silly songs. He bombed over and over again. People didn't get it. They booed. Any normal person would have walked away, but he kept going, and he didn't change. He kept up his weird routine. Other comedians told him to change, but he said no. For whatever reason, he knew he would make it.

"These people are idiots!" he'd tell the others backstage. "I'm hilarious." They thought he meant to say delirious.

But then it happened. *Saturday Night Live* came call-ing. Some producer or writer caught his act and saw potential. Sandler stuck to his guns and always per-formed what he thought was funny, even when no one else agreed. Now on television, he did the same weird schtick. Suddenly, everyone in the country laughed and sang along.

In the previous sections, you read about how I changed my vision for Parengo multiple times based on market demands. This was the right thing to do...for Parengo in a small town. It seems like a contradiction, and I don't know how to tell you to recognize the difference, but both decisions can lead to success.

Steve Jobs, Elon Musk, Michael Burry, Harland David Sanders, Sir James Dyson – so many people knew something to be their future, heard doubt, then succeeded anyway. Their vision carried them through. Equally true, many, many people started down a path with a vision, read the market, and changed accordingly in order to succeed. Perhaps they are two sides to the same coin. The vision coin, we'll call it.

One thing is certain: people who succeed have vision. Whether they plow ahead with one great idea or adapt to circumstances, successful people look at the world and see what could be. They remain a few steps ahead of the masses, inventing solutions before most people even know they have a problem. You will probably need to be adaptable in order to attract a small town market, but envisioning what your small town could be instead of what it always has been will be crucial to your success, no matter what industry you're in.

PASSING THE BATON

At some point, all things come to an end. Companies die or change hands every day. Even a brand as old as the hills hardly represents the same company as when it began.

"Pivoting" is the term we use when describing a major alteration in a business model or product line. Nintendo famously went from selling playing cards and other more random products and services to defining my childhood. Twitter, Instagram, Groupon, PayPal – they all started somewhere and eventually found their places somewhere else. My 20-year-old baristas spat venom at me recently when I said that YouTube will not last forever. They had never heard a more ridiculous sentence.

"I bet you said that about Netflix, too," one of them hissed at me, rolling her eyes to the foundation of her topknot.

It took me awhile to explain how I once hurried to my mailbox when I was their age to see if my new Netflix DVD had arrived, so that I could watch it and mail it back right away to get the most out of my $7.99. I'd spend half an hour every day perfecting my queue on their website, which was the first place I ever saw the word "queue." The same word cannot be found on the website today. Netflix pivoted into streaming. It will pivot again one day into something else. Then, in a far-off and dark future, it may not exist anymore.

As I finish this book, I am in the process of selling my coffee company. Early this year I received an offer for my wholesale assets and clients, and as the year closes, I am in discussion with a wonderful candidate to take over the café. Selling and pivoting are not the same thing, but they stir up some of the same scary feelings of change and uncertainty. It seems like my industry is changing all at once in my area. My good friends, The Abbotts, closed down their café, Cup 'n' Cork, a few months ago. The Ground-a-Bout is ever growing. Chad from Sweet Mayhem competes on television now. And Parengo will no longer belong to The Williams family.

Things change. The best thing you can do for your company and for your bank account is to hold on loosely – not too tight. As the underground racing sage, Twinkie, said, "If you ain't outta control, you ain't in control." When the market tells you to pivot, or when an offer pops up that would leave you happily unemployed, listen. It's no time to get sentimental. The new owners may change the style or take it in an unforeseen direction, but maybe they see something you don't. As long as your debts are paid, maybe it's time for you to walk away and start something new.

BETTER

You're not off the hook, yet.

Although the origin of this thought is attributed to Robert Baden-Powell, the founder of The Boy Scouts Association in the UK, Pinterest has toned it down for us:

"Leave everything better than you found it."

You opened your business with a head full of steam, and you made waves. You were a dynamo. You hosted events and volunteered and inspired and encouraged. For the first time people thought, hey, maybe this town is going places! That should come with some responsibility.

Before you take the money and run, reflect on your time with this company, with these people, with this town. Are you leaving it all better than before? Did you teach? Did you mentor? Did you learn? Did you receive criticism well? Were you kind? Neighborly?

I think of my town often. I did not live here long before I opened my shop, but it seems like it's a little better now. Certainly, people are drinking better coffee. Historic Downtown Sikeston is busier and more populated with new businesses and residences. More than 99% of this is not my doing, but Parengo was a part of it. We employed dozens over the years, displayed local art, played, learned, laughed, visited, maybe gave some folks a place to belong. One 100-year-old building is back in fighting shape after a facelift and some fresh paint. I got to spend a lot of quality time with my family and made some life-long friends in the process. That counts.

When the time for change arrives, make sure you can answer "yes" to some of these questions. Don't leave your family, friends, or patrons in debt. Fix the holes you put in the walls. Sweep up a little. Leave those who follow you with proper instruction and motivation to do even better than you did. Only then can you exit, on your way to something else. Plan to leave the next thing better than you found it, too.

THE END IN MIND

Knowing the end may come one day, you can plan for it now. Is the brand story you tell one that could leave your town better than you found it once you're gone? Does it contribute in some positive way every day to at least one part of your community? Take the piece of your business plan which we called "Exit Strategy" and combine it with your Architect Mask concepts from this section on branding to ensure that you are on your way to one day being able to pass the baton with your head held high.

ATTRACTING TALENT

Maybe you are not an entrepreneur, but you picked up this book in an effort to better understand what entrepreneurs want. You might be a City Manager or a Chamber of Commerce Director or a board member of a civic organization tasked with revitalizing a neighborhood. All around the country, leaders are realizing that by attracting entrepreneurs to their communities they are catalyzing growth and injecting their local economy with fuel.

You have a fresh batch of bright young minds in your local high schools and community colleges, but many of them will move away. Many just want regular lives with regular jobs and weekends free. Few of them will develop into thought-leading entrepreneurs who could change the fabric of your community. And so it should be. Entrepreneurship is not for everyone. If you care about your students' futures at all, then teach the majority of them how to write code or to weld underwater. They will be the most employable class in the world.

So then, most of those around you are not entrepreneurially minded. That means you have to go out and find some folks who are. They are out there! They are writing business plans, editing their Kickstarter videos, searching YouTube for how to edit a Kickstarter video. Their ears are piqued for whispers of good opportunity.

Why you? Why us? Why this town? We think this, and we are defeated. We go back to kicking the dead horse of "how things used to be" and beating our heads against the wall of "we have to work together to get this thing going."

It is a good point, though. Why would an entrepreneur with a bazillion dollar idea move to your town? What's in it for her? Is your town better than other options? Historic buildings, inexpensive storefronts, and up-and-coming neighborhoods are available in small towns across the country. You need something more.

Think of it like dating. You're a guy. You want to ask this entrepreneur and her business to grab a coffee and then move in with your forever. Only, you're not the only one asking. Other small towns want her too. This is an attractive business we're talking about! She could date anyone she wants. She could stay right where she is and work things out. She could even run into the arms of a rich, more experienced man – a city. Maybe you're in good shape. Maybe you're not too smart, and you have no sense of humor, but you sure are pretty, and you have retained an enviable head of hair. You may just have a shot at this, but you need to get creative.

You go for it, and she likes you. You're charming and hospitable. She moves in. Things are going great! You decide to relax. Dating was hard work, and you put in a lot of time and energy. Now you can finally slip into some sweatpants and watch The Wire like you always wanted to. Start at the beginning! Make yourself some nachos! Let your guard down for once! You know how this story ends.

The point is this: become a town worth living in, moving to, and investing with. If you are a loser and remain a loser, no one will date you. If you are cool at first but let yourself go, she will leave. Don't be a loser town.

Just like in the dating world, becoming an attractive town is not only about improving your physical appearance. Beautification is nice, but culture, heritage, diversity, innovation, and financial incentive are especially appealing. Think of how many cash-strapped startups would notice your town if it offered small business grants and tax breaks or ultra-fast Wi-Fi or plush office spaces for which the starting rent is $1 per month for new businesses.

Across America, small towns are adapting to wrap their minds around their entrepreneurial ecosystems.

They are thinking creatively about how to import the next generation in a time when populations flock to cities worldwide. The tactics are never exactly the same, but by learning from each other, we can gain inspiration to put our towns into the next big headlines.

In May 2016, I spoke with Adam Plagge, who was then the Executive Director of the Fairfield Economic Development Association (FEDA) in Fairfield, Iowa. Ask most people who have been plugged into the entrepreneurial world for a while, and Fairfield will be one of the first examples they give as a small town doing big things. For twenty years now, Fairfield has been the standard of excellence of towns doing what you are setting out to do. Here's a short Q&A with Mr. Plagge to help get your town's creative juices flowing:

What did Fairfield do to encourage its startup culture?

There have been several attempts to incubate new businesses in Fairfield over the years. FEDA constructed an industrial spec building that housed two companies, Traf-Fix Devices and H&H Molding - affiliated with Agri-Industrial Plastics in the 1990s. Both companies are now ingrained in the local economy working closely with local companies and employing more than 60 employees.

FEDA also helped found the Fairfield CoLab - a 5,000 square foot co-working space downtown - to help create a technology community and collaborative environment.

Last year FEDA also began hosting a business pitch competition and venture capital event to help local entrepreneurs attract funding. The two winners of last year's competition received cash prizes and were helped integrate into the community through partnerships with the local hospital, who is an early adopter of Punctil Health (another Fairfield startup), and the city entered into a favorable lease agreement for a vacant building with Red Cannon Expedition for their new business venture.

How did other forces contribute to the entrepreneurial ecosystem (state government, economic development organizations, civic organizations, corporations, CIDs, TIFFs or Historic Districting, grants, etc.)?

The Fairfield Entrepreneurial Association has also been a long-time facilitator of economic gardening in the community. The Chamber of Commerce helped create a low-interest loan program in conjunction with local lenders for new businesses in the downtown district. Area 15, our regional COG, and Access Energy have lent out hundreds of thousands of dollars through its revolving loan fund to new and expanding businesses in Fairfield.

Who led the change?

Businesses like Agri-Industrial Plastics, Iowa State Bank, and Cambridge have played large roles in building out community amenities such as the Convention Center and the new Park and Recreation Facility. Lori Schaefer-Weaton of Agri has played a large role in Project Lead the Way and ABI, helping encourage the new generation of Advanced Manufacturing in Fairfield. Other business leaders like Tommy Thompson of TD&T Accounting and Ed Malloy of Danaher Oil have played important civic roles, helping run the city while also creating new jobs.

Is growth in any other culture within a town a direct correlate to entrepreneurship?

A number of cultural elements need to come together to create an environment in which entrepreneurs can thrive. A vibrant arts, music, and restaurant scene definitely contributed to Fairfield's ability to attract and retain entrepreneurial talent and the workforce needed to drive new business growth.

If a small town with debt, stagnation, or general decline wants to embrace entrepreneurship, encourage innovation, and attract businesses, what should it do?

A catalyst for change is essential. In Fairfield we already had a rich history of entrepreneurship. However, the influx of highly educated individuals moving to Fairfield to take part in the movement helped create a resurgence and influx of capital investment. This created a unique and fertile environment for a rural Iowa community. This is a difficult scenario to recreate but if a rural community can attract talent through a high quality of life, can create a strong coalition of community leaders, and can differentiate itself in some fashion, then it can be accomplished.

THE BACKSTORY

By the end of the '90s, Fairfield already had a reputation for embracing the ideas which the rest of us are just now discovering. Known as "Silicorn Valley," Fairfield attracted the attention of *The New York Times* [5] for its ability to entice entrepreneurs from out of town and to cultivate startup culture. It still receives national attention for its methods, its success stories, and its unique features – such as Maharishi University – even though its population hovers around 10,000.

---

[5] Andrew Bluth, "Hot Spots/Silicorn Valley," 1998, The New York Times, 23 June 2015 <https://www.nytimes.com/1998/09/23/business/hot-spots-silicorn-valley-meditating-for-fun-and-profit.html>.

CHAPTER TWELVE

ADAPT

You're getting into this now. You didn't realize how much of an entrepreneur you were before, but now you recognize that voice that has been screaming in the back of your skull. I'll say it again: too often small town businesses embrace the standards of the small business. But YOU ARE AN ENTREPRENEUR!

If it is true that you already own or run a business but that many of these entrepreneurial lessons are new to you, then it may also be true that you are completely disgusted with your brand at this point. You didn't create it with much intention, and now that you have an idea of the story you would like it to tell, it nags at you. Every day you walk in and hate the music you play, the logo looks like a big hairy mole on the façade, and those blog posts you wrote two years ago make you want to puke.

It might be time to adapt or pivot. Rebranding is a common practice, and it does not mean that something is wrong or that a business is failing. Rebranding does not equate with weakness. Things change. Your brand can too.

David Brier of DBD International helps companies build brands, but he also works with companies of all sizes to rebuild their brands. It happens all the time, and hundreds of companies like Brier's exist to consult on this process. I believe the key question Brier asks clients is, "If we were starting our business today, would this be the brand solution we would come up with?" Brier illustrates the feeling you may have now: "For some, it happens early on once they've discovered *who they really are*, while with others, it occurs after many years of having grown (or outgrown) their brand."[6] You are in good and plentiful company.

As an added obstacle, entrepreneurs in small towns must look at rebranding in a different light than our urban contemporaries. Since there is no startup culture, normal practices of rebranding experts may not work here. It could be considered almost common for a tech business to restructure, pivot its product line or service offerings, release a new logo, and change its name. On another level, the press generated by Pepsi's logo changes are worth the cost of changing the logo every now and then – even if the feedback is bad.

[6] David Brier, "How to Rebrand: 19 Questions to Ask Before You Start," DBD International, 11 May 2018 <https://www.risingabovethenoise. com/how-to-rebrand-19-questions-ask-before-you-start/>.

Small town entrepreneurs cannot rely on the same amount of splash. Often, we simply don't have the money to do it like the big boys. Still, sometimes we know our businesses are not saying what we want them to say. Therefore, we must consider ways to steer our brand stories without breaking ourselves in the process. So, deconstruct your story. Go in reverse order. What are the end, the middle, and the beginning? What are the pieces that have worked up until now, and what do I need to change moving forward?

Even if you never need to rebrand your business (maybe your brand rocks, your customers are loyal, and your website is bangin'), you should frequently consider what every facet of your business is saying about your brand story. It is easy for one piece to get away from the rest of the puzzle. Three types of branding problems happen often in small towns, and entrepreneurs need to keep careful watch in order to work a special kind of rebranding into their practices. Let's take a look at each of these:

1) All Ships Rise

2) Sam's Rule

3) The World in Burgers

ALL SHIPS RISE – A DOWNTOWN SIKESTON TALE

By 2013, Historic Downtown Sikeston became interesting enough to attract me and my coffee company, but in those early days it was clear that the neighborhood had a long way to go. We knew the amount of existing traffic would be enough to sustain the shop, but it was nowhere near enough to create an empire. Downtown still occupied a vague place in the local hivemind. Everyone knew it was there, had always been, would always be, but few bothered to venture too near. I decided right away that half of my task (aka, my second full-time job) would be to develop the neighborhood. I could see the future: nightlife, apartments, public art, a latte in every hand. I thought that by creating a culture in which Parengo Coffee was the heart and soul, I could attract a steady flow of the cappuccino drinking demographics to my front door. I sincerely hoped to benefit others in the neighborhood at the same time. All ships rise – you know the saying.

One of our local PEO chapters met in my shop. They asked me to talk about my business, Downtown, and its progress. I asked them what they thought. Have you noticed a difference down here? These are opinion leaders, women of affluence and education. If they take notice, then we are getting somewhere, and others will hear about it. Hands shot up around the room.

In order to help people to believe in our neighborhood, and in order to believe in it ourselves, we needed a visual aid. This came in the form of *BRINK Magazine*. Toward the end of 2014, I collected a menagerie of creative regulars from my shop and asked them to help me build an arts, entertainment, food, and lifestyle quarterly for the neighborhood. Every city is covered by several free magazines like this, so why couldn't we do that here? Everyone agreed that we probably could. It didn't look too hard. We partnered with a local printer, sold ads to Downtown merchants like myself, and got busy creating content. Ashton, our town's best graphic designer and roller derby wunderkind, agreed to lay it out and handle ad design. Ashton introduced me to Mallory, a freelance photographer with zero photojournalism interests. Somehow, after a ten-minute conversation, Mallory agreed to abandon her principles and be the only photographer for an entire magazine. Together, they made our Downtown sizzle, even when it still lacked luster in real life. Alex wanted to write about food and music, Cameron conducted interviews with business owners, and other leaders in our town gladly contributed columns. A month later, we passed out 2000 copies of a gorgeous, full color, 48-page publication that made our Downtown look like the neighborhood we all wanted it to be. It popped. It shone brilliant on every page. Miles away, people flipped through our pages and started paying attention.

We used *BRINK* to illustrate the Downtown we wanted, not necessarily the one that existed yet. In our second issue, the cover story focused on Downtown living. The second floors above our storefronts are a huge wasted opportunity. People who live directly above a store never have to drive and park in order to shop there. We read that residents of a business or shopping district are more likely to spend a good chunk of their income in that neighborhood, and we wanted to show Sikeston how that could look Downtown, so we displayed cool people and their cool apartments. Only seven people lived Downtown at the time, but we left that detail out. Readers saw beautiful images of young professionals who adored their lofts and their neighborhood. Suddenly, the seeds were planted, and I began to hear rumors of property owners who suddenly were interested in renovating their empty second stories.

Around that time, I presented our magazine to the Tri-State Advertising and Marketing Professionals group in Cape Girardeau, Missouri. At the end of the meeting, one member told me, "I want to move someplace new, and I've always avoided Sikeston like the plague, but now I think I have to start looking at homes there." If she becomes a regular coffee drinker, then it was worth the twenty minutes I spent editing that article.

This has been a story of the rebranding of a neighborhood. It may seem tangential. We need to focus on our businesses, so enough with the neighborhood stuff! Fine, but not everyone who figures out how to relaunch a great new brand concept can pick up and move out of an unsupportive neighborhood. Sometimes, you have to get creative. Every story needs a setting. Batman can only exist in Gotham. The journey of hobbits only makes sense when they're traversing Middlearth, and Harry had to go to Hogwarts. Your brand story is no exception. Some energy aimed at cultivating your town or neighborhood immediately contributes to the awareness of your brand by virtue of proximity.

Some days, it feels like Parengo Coffee and Downtown Sikeston are synonyms. People say they want to drive down and see the new mural above Grant Financial, and that includes stopping in my shop, eating lunch at Susie's, window shopping at Margaret & James, checking the deals at Paul's or Bo's or Personal Expressions, and finishing the night at Jeremiah's. Parengo without Downtown probably would not have worked. It took me putting work into both efforts in order for my ship to rise with the rest.

SAM'S RULE

Have you ever seen a photo of your aunt when she was 22 years old? Is she embarrassed by it? Go find a picture of yourself from junior high. Better yet, go look up AC Slater from *Saved By The Bell*. Someone thought the coolest guy in the coolest group of friends at the coolest public school in America should wear those pants, and every girl in the country agreed with resounding adoration. Now, look at those pants! What are those pants?! Imagine if Mario Lopez still dressed that way.

A former marine owns a jewelry store in my neighborhood. His name is Sam. He remodels his business every three years. He totally overhauls the store. A crew comes in and rips out everything down to the studs and brick and concrete, and Sam works with local builders to design a whole new look that represents who and what his business is today. He believes that three years is the perfect amount of time in which a place can feel fresh. Any longer and the business looks stale. Businesses who never freshen up can sometimes retain their charm, but too often they end up suffering from the interior design equivalent of "He's still wearing that?!"

Remodeling every three years may be the perfect pattern for Sam and his jewelry business, but it may not be right for you. Even so, do not put all the hard work into opening a beautiful store or office or food truck and then coasting the rest of your life. We already agreed that, even in small towns, people are up to date on trends. If you were a citizen of the moment in 2015 and coated the inside of your home décor store in shiplap – you might've even made a pilgrimage to Waco – then you could wake up one day and wonder why you thought that looked so good back then. It might be a smart practice to browse around other stores within your industry every few years for signs of change. Your brand could be dependent on the image that you are up on the latest trends. This principle applies to aspects of your business beyond interior design. Even when every other part of your company is clicking, an old-fashioned font or color or texture or slogan can make customers begin the swift process of losing interest. Don't give them the chance.

In Sam's case, people talk about the remodel. When the business is closed for a few days for the renovation, people talk about it. When trucks pull up with new display cases, people talk about it. When it reopens, people talk about it. And when Sam throws a party to christen the new look, people show up. They take pictures and post them online. Even if you only walk into his jewelry store every three years or so, it will look brand-spanking new every time, and you will probably feel good about spending your money there.

THE WORLD IN BURGERS

One summer, I taught American football for a few weeks in Poland. In my life, I have barely played American football, but being American, I am qualified to teach it in some capacity in Poland. Eastern Europe is lovely, and I very much enjoyed my time there and all of the wonderful people. However, the food sucked.

After twenty hours of flying on the cheapest routes possible, with plenty of layovers and transfers to save a few bucks, I then followed it up by three hours of riding shotgun next to a Polish man who picked me up from the airport and then drove 1000 kilometers per hour through round-a-bouts which included signs advertising that intersection's death toll. I was sweaty, terrified, excited, and deep in the throes of travel hunger. Finally, plopping down in the cafeteria at sports camp, I greedily shook the hands of my mates for the season and even more greedily poured myself a heaping bowl of Coo-oooookie Crisp. Plus milk. Can't forget the milk. I practically dumped the bowl down my own gullet.

It is funny how broken expectations suddenly heighten our senses. A split second before the breakfast hit my tongue, I somehow became aware that the milk was nearly body temperature. Also, it held a viscosity that I cannot forget. I do not remember if it was goat's milk or cow's milk, but I imagine they exit the body at the same rate when spat back into one's chocolate chip cereal bowl.

Luckily, it was almost lunchtime on Friday anyways. I got cleaned up, ate a Lion Bar from the canteen, and hustled back to get my gut on Poland time. Friday lunches, so they told me, are rooted in a culinary tradition that dates back centuries. Another version of the story told that the meal I was about to eat had nostalgic roots associated with communist rations and the appreciation of a post-communist Poland. Whatever the actual reason, the retired women who ran this camp's kitchen followed dogmatic Polish cafeteria customs. So, I should've seen lunch coming somehow. Again, I tucked in heartily. Someone spooned a steaming, wiggling bowl of rotini noodles in front of me. Another lady then poured the pasta sauce from a great height with skill that revealed her decades of practice. This pinkish, off-putting sauce was noticeably NOT steaming like the noodles, but I was up for anything at this point, so I slurped it up.

Did you know a traditional Polish dish is chilled strawberry soup on pasta? I didn't either. The strawberry "sauce" is roughly the texture, flavor, and appearance of a strawberry smoothie. I ate Lion Bars every Friday for lunch for the rest of the summer.

Life is optimism for food-loving people. There's always another meal coming up, and we are looking forward to them. So, after a week or two, I heard a rumor that one of the staff members made frequent trips to town and always stopped at McDonald's. Yes, there was a McDonald's, even in a tiny town in the middle of nowhere in Poland.

One day, I stole a ride. After hot days of American football and candy for lunch, this was like walking into *Le Bernardin*. The catch is: on the local food scene, that is not much of an exaggeration. It seemed almost fancy, to my surprise and delight. I later learned that it was one of the nicest restaurants in town because of a number of adaptations the company made when expanding to this part of Europe. McDonald's in Poland is, reportedly, a great place to work, with high wages and benefits. The place was spotless, and it smelled like love. The menu listed less than ten items. The thick patties hung off the sides of freshly baked buns, and fresh, regional produce made up the toppings and sides. Locals considered it expensive. I bummed many rides into town that summer.

One would think McDonald's figured out long ago the singular recipe that would ensure success across every border, race, creed, or climate, but even they have to adapt to each market in order to stand out. Even within one market, tastes change. Gone are the days of Playplaces. We now see espresso machines inside the drive-thru windows. Happy Meals can now include apple slices, and "artisan" appears on the menu several times. They know how to adapt.

When you opened your business, you were the new, hot thing in town. People loved your cupcakes and commented on that light fixture and told you that you should definitely open one in the town next door. You expanded. You have three or four locations now, but none of your markets responded exactly like that first one, and even your longtime original customers are starting to ask for recipes they saw on Pinterest. So, consider what McDonald's did! Each town might be different. Some places love sweet tea, and some love unsweet tea. Some like ranch, and some like mustard. What you offer down to the condiments and the logos on the napkins tells your brand's story, and that story may change place-to-place or year-to-year. You are your story's teller. Figure out how to tell it well, no matter who is listening.

SMALL TOWNS, REVISITED

By now, I hope you share my conviction that small towns are primed for entrepreneurship. In small towns, we know about trends faster than ever before. Social media and other technologies provide immediate demand and almost unlimited scalability. Plus, everything is less expensive in a small town, so an entrepreneur's overhead is less than his big city competitor's.

Whether you are an entrepreneur already, considering becoming one, or positioned as a leader in your small town, there are some other unique characteristics of today's small town that beg contemplation. In his great book, Bowling Alone, Robert D. Putnam highlights how towns across America are seeing the collapse of civic organizations and a drastic decline in the willingness of citizens to donate to or to volunteer for local efforts. The concept of family is no longer homogenous. More seek work-from-home and "no collar" jobs. Every change requires adaptation from leaders and provides opportunity for entrepreneurs.

COMPLEX RELATIONSHIPS

The author Lance Schaubert writes on his website about how, in cities, a person knows another person for one reason only. "That's the guy where I get my bagels." In a small town, relationships are splintered, duplicated, layered, and much more complex. The bagel guy is also your attorney's son, and you remember when he was in high school with your cousin and gave you a ride to church every Sunday one summer. Schaubert writes that "in a small town, the burden of society is shared by fewer people." [7] We each wear many hats.

So, as we acknowledge the many changes taking place in our small towns, we cannot simply scowl or ignore it. Our relationships are too intertwined not to welcome the change - to try to understand it at least. Moreover, as entrepreneurs, any changes and our intimate connections to those involved offer new and exciting needs for our businesses to fill.

DO THE UNDONE

As important as it is to know how your town is and how it has been, do not hesitate to dream about how

[7] Lance Schaubert, "The Beautiful Complexity of a Tiny Town," 2017, LanceSchaubert.org, 21 Feb. 2017 <http://lanceschaubert.org/2017/02/21/tiny-town-break-up-in-a-small-town/>.

it could be. You may be the creative force who inspires your town to morph into something revolutionary. At one time, Fairfield, Iowa or that exceptional small town near you were unknown, unimpressive, and unexceptional. Someone envisioned what they could be and inspired others to follow.

Your small town may have a unique characteristic. In that case, it's a no-brainer! Embrace your weird and run with it. However, if you struggle to find something attractive about your town, maybe you could try something novel.

Years ago, Paducah, Kentucky found itself with a struggling neighborhood full of homes which were noticeably going into disrepair. Leaders developed an idea to sell these homes to working artists, often for as little as $1, and a local bank stepped in to provide financing. Even when appraisals looked bleak, bankers and developers invested in what could be.[8] Now, eighteen years after initiating the project, Paducah is known in its region for its vibrant arts culture. Entrepreneurs followed. In the past few years, Paducah added breweries, restaurants, coffee shops, galleries, and a Mellow Mushroom. Forward-thinking civic leaders invested in a niche of entrepreneurs – artists – and now it's paying off.

[8] Mary Campbell, "Lessons from Paducah, KY," 2017, Cape Breton Spectator, 2 July 2018 <https://capebretonspectator.com/2017/02/15/paducah-kentucky-artist-relocate/>.

TWO IDEAS YOU CAN HAVE FOR FREE

Many states neglect to include film tax incentives into their yearly budgets. States like Georgia, which is now one of the best places in the world to make movies, offer arrangements that benefit filmmakers and local businesses mutually, bringing thousands of employed people through the state each year. Entire economies spring up around studios and projects in towns that welcome film crews and fans alike.

Your state may not offer incentives like this, but what if your town did? Film shoots require dozens, hundreds, or sometimes thousands of people. Think of the required taxes, lodging, food, insurance, construction, clothing, medical care, and entertainment needed to keep an operation like that going. If your town contributed to some of those costs, offering tax breaks or grants, free locations and a welcoming populace, and recruited filmmakers and their crews, think of the economic impact! Entrepreneurs would dream up thousands of ways to support this industry and to create wealth in your Small Movietown, USA.

The next 50 years are expected to see mass human migration around the globe. Already, refugee camps are overflowing, and border predicaments threaten to become unsolvable. A lot of gut reactions are saying, "I'm glad that's not happening here." But what if your town said the opposite? What if your town said, "Need a new home? You're welcome here!" Host families could invite relocators into their homes from crises around the world, providing family and a place to belong. Yes, the new faces would bring a lot of differences, but that includes new food, new skills, new products, new music, new spices and stories and customs. Think of the ripples in the local marketplace! Grocers and restaurants would open or expand to accommodate. The new members of your community would bring skills and educations from previous careers, and some of them are bound to be entrepreneurs. Your town would make headlines around the world, and your entrepreneurs would have a heyday.

Your town is special – if not for an obvious reason, then simply because you are there. People are always looking for a place to fit in and to call home. Many may feel right at home in your town with a little dose of you thinking outside the box.

CHAPTER THIRTEEN

THE INTERNET

I'll never be mistaken for a fashionista. Start talking to me about hair and makeup and watch me fall asleep before your eyes. Seriously, I'll drop like I have narcolepsy, right into my coffee mug. I'll be burned. You'll have to call an ambulance.

I like to have one good pair of footwear. Keep your sneakers. Give me a broken-in pair of leather chukkas or some Timberland work boots, and I don't want anything else in my closet. I wear them until they literally fall apart beyond repair.

That's just something people say, right? "Wear them until they fall apart beyond repair"? No, I mean it! I know they are beyond repair, because I go to Bob's and beg him to fix them for me. When he says, "Can't do nothin' for 'em." – that's how I know it is time to buy a new pair of boots.

I feel so strongly about my boots, because years ago I began an absurd screenplay about footwear. As part of my research, I asked Bob to allow me into his workshop. He graciously let me into the inner sanctum, where I watched him stretch leather and stitch and buff and polish. I had no idea so much went into shoes.

Prior to this experience, shoes were just shoes. I threw them in the closet or kicked them across the room. I never thought about shoelaces until they broke. I needed shoes, but I didn't care about them. Then I walked into Bob's.

Bob's Shoe Service is a small business in Cape Girardeau, Missouri, about thirty miles from my house. The workshop consists of rows of ancient wooden tables and racks, each covered in gashes as if Bob secretly swordfights in his spare time. A thick layer of every color of polish dapples each surface from the floor to the ceiling. Imagine a beach ball full of multi-colored meringue burst and splattered the room, and it all dried that way. Strips of leather hang over a wire next to a wall full of gouges, scissors, knives, pliers, punches, needles, hammers, awls, and clamps. One tabletop rolls back to reveal a puck of every polish ever made. Another exposes reel after reel of thread in every hue the human eye can see. Bob himself moves among the stations with a deftness and ability that leaves me with one conclusion: he definitely swordfights. It's all very impressive and cool.

Yeah, this chapter is about the Internet. Much like shoes, the Internet made up a tiny part of most of my life, but I never thought much about it. Yes, it's all very cool, and I can watch movies late at night and look up the difference between effect and affect, but when it comes down to making money, the Internet is not my realm. I didn't know what to do there. It took a Bob's Shoe Service-esque experience to make me understand how the small town entrepreneur should be thinking about the Internet.

SMALL TOWN INTERNET 1.0

Many small town entrepreneurs realize that everyone is online. So, we put our businesses online. We hope people will find us online and come to us to spend money. We try to be engaging with photos and videos and contests so that more people will like, share, and comment but all for the same purpose. Activity on our pages makes us look popular and reputable, and that leads to people making the decision to physically come to us to spend money.

A lot of us also realize that ad money spent online goes a lot further than ad money spent in the real world. There are some small businesses in my town who kill it with print, television, and radio commercials still. They spend upwards of $50,000 per year in traditional media, and they make it back threefold, at least. For those of us whose target demographics are middle-aged or younger, however, we get more bang for our buck online.

Very few of us invest in online sales. Setting up an e-commerce platform, hiring someone to take product photos, design ads, update inventory, etc. – it can get expensive. Plus, it takes a lot of time, which many of us don't have. We hustling individuals are our own CEOs, marketing departments, photographers, and custodians. There are no more minutes in the day for doing a quality job online. However, if we can pick up a few extra dollars through our websites with minimal effort, we'll try it out.

Until now, that's how we have used the Internet. It's another place to hang a sign in the hopes that people will get offline and walk in our doors. We dipped our toes into it as a revenue stream, but we already have these great businesses out here in the real world, right?! Hopefully, people will see our websites, come to their senses, unplug everything, and come live a real life out here with us.

SMALL TOWN INTERNET 2.0

Recently, my aforementioned, nomadic, sometimes-roommate Ashley passed through Missouri again. While here, she invited me to learn about a deeper level of Internet, of which she happens to be an expert. Actually, it was more like she kicked my legs out from under me and shoved my head into a toilet until I could hardly breathe. As I came up, gasping for air, I screamed, "Tell me more!" It was my Red Pill Moment.

Did you know there are teenagers making $9,000 per month online? Neither did I. These are not isolated cases – there are a lot of them. I can't write the book on how to get rich online, and this is not an attempt to do so. The person who should write that book is probably in eleventh grade. However, I can boil it down into this: the Internet Titans keep detailed records of everything that happens online, and that data is available to you with a few clicks. By working blogs or social media daily, by presenting targeted messages to niche markets, and by doubling down on your brand story, you can add a gigantic revenue stream to your business.

Small town Internet 2.0 is about realizing that the Internet is not just about bringing people to our businesses. It is about taking our businesses to the people. The Internet allows you to reach to the other side of the globe and not just to the Interstate. With concepts like drop shipping, click funneling, and order fulfillment, you can sell your products without ever going to the post office, or you can sell other products to the market you've already established without any production overhead.

I spent five years carving out a market and building local brand recognition with Parengo. Now, we are in the process of building up that momentum online. Our Facebook and Instagram followers exude passion for our coffee, and with a few clicks, we can see that they are mostly 25-44-year old females with some college education. Another large portion are 35-44-year old men who like the outdoors – hunting, fishing, camping, biking, or sports. By targeting ads and posts to a specific niche – like "men who camp" – and by offering products that 1) they might like, 2) fit our brand, and 3) we already love – such as our "Camper's Pour Over Set" – we are able to hit volume numbers that our shop could never do in our small town. Shoppers from all over the country click on our site and buy our products, then the manufacturers fulfill the orders and ship directly to the buyers. Small Town Internet 2.0 provides low-risk, high-reward revenue streams to any type of entrepreneur willing to take the time to learn it.

EMBRACE IT

Do you see the implications? We've already discussed this, but again, people want to live in our towns. We have a lifestyle and amenities that many entrepreneurs desire. Those entrepreneurs employ people who want it, too. From owning affordable, income-producing land to great schools and Friday night football games, to outdoor recreation and the slower pace of rural habits, thousands of small towns look like beautiful options for entrepreneurs, if only they could make the same amount of money there. Now, by putting the Internet to work for us, just like the big dogs do in the cities, we can live anywhere we want!

Small towns should embrace this. Realize what entrepreneurs want and invest in it. My town offers some of the least expensive electricity in Missouri, thanks to our power plant. What if we also offered the fastest, most affordable Internet in the Midwest and free city-wide Wi-Fi? Our Downtown organization provides group advertising perks to member businesses, but what if we also hired an expert to put every one of our members online and to run their targeted ad campaigns? The more creative and forward-thinking a small town can get on this subject, the more it will see entrepreneurs choosing to do business and to build lives in its care.

PART V
CONCLUDING REMARKS

CHAPTER FOURTEEN

CONCLUSION: THE ENTREPRENEUR

We live in an era of entrepreneurs. We talk more about Elon Musk than about Tesla or SpaceX. If Musk launches a new venture, we pay attention, not primarily because of the company, but because Elon Musk owns it. We remember Steve Jobs now on the level of mythological hero. Can you imagine if Alfred Hitchcock or Orson Welles had made movies about the origins of Gillette or Marlboro? Can you even name the people who founded those companies? No! But in our time, the Facebook story wins Academy Awards, and more people recognize Mark Zuckerberg than they do David Fincher, who made the film. It is the sexiest age in history to be labeled an entrepreneur.

Our particular type of madness leads us to fantasize about being next. Remember the Optimism Bias? We see ourselves on the covers of magazines, all our plans working out, cashing in one endeavor to fund the next one. Luckily for you and for me, now is the best time to go for it, because now is the best time we will ever have to be an entrepreneur. In your small town, you will make the news. You will be invited to speak, to teach, to train, to sit on the board. You will be able to buy property, to dream big, and to execute those dreams for relatively little cost. This is your era.

Don't let that hinder you, though. These principles and practices of successful entrepreneurs in small towns will help you build an empire that can last. Healthy companies run by healthy people with healthy teams succeed whether or not the era is favorable toward entrepreneurial celebrity. In order to build that company, you must work. You must master the basics. You must tell a great story. Then, you might be next.

SEAT OF CHAIR MOMENTS

Mary Heaton Vorse said, "The art of writing is the art of applying the seat of the pants to the seat of the chair." She meant to convince her writing pupils that in order to be a writer, one must write. The literal act of doing a thing is the only way to get that thing done.

There is so much talk in the entrepreneurship world. Charismatic preppies with all the right Burning Man connections seem to pop up frequently with Series A funding or IPO rumors, while I can't for the life of me decipher what their companies even do. Small town folks are skeptical of the buzzwords and the snake oil salesmen. They respect effort and sincerity.

So, while big dreams might be your reality in the future, I challenge you to embrace the time it takes to get there. Seek Seat of Chair moments every day. Get down to the work of doing the work, and eventually you will see progress. Vacuum. Interview. Reconcile the bank accounts. Cold call one more number. Every Seat of Chair moment that you grab hold of becomes another brick that you lay down. One day, those bricks become a building. One day, two. One day, you just may have an empire.

ACKNOWLEDGEMENTS

I couldn't do anything without my parents, Larry & Theda Williams. They're the coolest. They're the reasons people come into the shop and hang out every day. They pulled me along through lots of weeds and made Parengo possible. All my best friends and family who are mentioned in these pages and who read my earliest drafts - Jason Santiago, Kate Austin, Ashley Hayes, Lance Schaubert, Glenn Landberg, Joe Boudreau, Noelle Kwan, Cameron Godwin, Jay & Camille Lancaster – I would've abandoned this a long time ago without your help. And thanks for letting me tell stories about you. Ashton Schlitt, Mallory Due, Derek Hammeke, Mark Neuenschwander, Kara Kaminsky - Parengo's brand is as much yours as it is mine. Thank you for saying yes to most of my crazy ideas. I get so much support from these people, I can't even begin to express my gratitude.

People who are way smarter than me let me bounce ideas off of them and talk through these chapters from the very beginning of the idea. Steve Rice, Calvin Friedrich, Jakob Pallesen, Brian Tapp, Johann Stuntebeck, Jason Duff – when any of you decide to write a book, I will be the first to buy it.

To those who contributed chapters or answers to polls or who helped make my time in Missouri and in Downtown Sikeston great, thanks so much. You're all way better at this than me, so thank you for letting me watch and learn. Becky McCray, Bob Schooley, Carissa Stark, Mackenzie Price, Joe Recker, Emilie Stephens, Anthony Cervantes, Lynn Lancaster, Laurie Everett, Michael Haugh, Marc Leible, Sam Thomas, I look up to you all.

To everyone who has ever been with the MIC, the SBTDC, and the DRA, I've had the best time working with you and getting to know you. Thank you for every email, every demographic tapestry, letter of recommendation, and great conversation. To the Delta Entrepreneurship Network Fellows class of 2015, I hope you're still awesome and changing the world every day. To everyone in Historic Downtown Sikeston, you created a beautiful and really fun neighborhood. Keep going.

And to everyone who ever bought a cup of Parengo Coffee, thank you. This one's for you.

QUESTIONS YOU SHOULD BE ASKING

What's a need I could fill?

Why am I starting a business?

Who is my ideal customer?

What could I change if all my customers end up being people I did not anticipate? Am I willing to change those things?

Is anyone's life better because my business exists?

What's the most important thing I want a customer to tell a friend ten minutes after doing business with me?

What's the most important thing I want a visitor to tell a friend ten days after visiting my town?

How does my staff relate to each other? What do they need from each other and from me?

How does my staff relate to customers? What does each party get out of the interaction?

What role do I serve in my community?

What are five words I want to see repeated when people describe my business online, in reviews, to friends, or in print?

Where are the next five towns in which I could duplicate my business? Or, which five towns will I expand to next?

What type of person, personality, or skill set do I need to hire next to make my team more complete?

What type of person becomes a fan and not just a customer?

What does the path look like that people must go down in order to go from hearing about my company to patronizing it regularly? How often do they see or hear my ads? How are they treated along that path by me or my staff? What interaction made the difference?

What does it feel like to walk in my door for the first time? What do I want it to feel like?

What extracurricular groups or events could I participate in in order to make myself and my business essential to the social fabric of my town?

What is something weird or unique about my business that I did not plan but that I could now embrace?

How do I spend my time every day in five-minute increments? What could I change to become more efficient? More profitable? Healthier? A better friend or family member?

Which parts of my business, equipment, time, or building are underutilized? How could I add an additional revenue stream?

What did I do well today?

What task do I do every day that I could reimagine to do more efficiently? Could I invent something to make this happen?

Which part of my business could I repackage to increase its scalability?

What am I buying from a supplier that I could begin supplying to others?

Does my logo say what I want it to say?

What is a good metaphor for my business?

Where are my customers? What do they do? What do they read or look at every day? What types of jokes or news or pretty pictures do they share? How can I become an integral part of that?

How would my neighborhood have to change in order for my business to grow? How can I get creative and make those changes happen?

What will my town be like in five or ten years? Will the people change? What will they want by that time? How can I prepare to be the one who offers it first and best?

Who are the next leaders in my town or on my staff? How can I help them realize their full potential?

FOOTNOTES

[1] Nick Bilton, "Elizabeth Holmes, Somehow, is Trying to Start a New Company," 2018, Vanity Fair Hive, 13 Sept. 2018 <https://www.vanityfair.com/news/2018/06/elizabeth-holmes-is-trying-to-start-a-new-company>.

[2] Covey, S. The Seven Habits of Highly Effective People. (New York: Simon and Schuster, 1989).

[3] <Bcorporation.net>

[4] Amy Patterson Neubert, "Money Only Buys Happiness for a Certain Amount," 2018, Purdue University News, 20 Aug. 2018 <https://www.purdue.edu/newsroom/releases/2018/Q1/money-only-buys-happiness-for-a-certain-amount.html>.

[5] Andrew Bluth, "Hot Spots/Silicorn Valley," 1998, The New York Times, 23 June 2015 <https://www.nytimes.com/1998/09/23/business/hot-spots-silicorn-valley-meditating-for-fun-and-profit.html>.

[6] David Brier, "How to Rebrand: 19 Questions to Ask Before You Start," DBD International, 11 May 2018 <https://www.risingabovethenoise.com/how-to-rebrand-19-questions-ask-before-you-start/>.

[7] Lance Schaubert, "The Beautiful Complexity of a Tiny Town," 2017, LanceSchaubert.org, 21 Feb. 2017 <http://lanceschaubert.org/2017/02/21/tiny-town-break-up-in-a-small-town/>.

[8] Mary Campbell, "Lessons from Paducah, KY," 2017, Cape Breton Spectator, 2 July 2018 <https://capebretonspectator.com/2017/02/15/paducah-kentucky-artist-relocate/>.

ABOUT THE AUTHOR

Colby Williams and his parents founded Parengo Coffee in Sikeston, Missouri in 2013. He won a Delta Entrepreneurship Network Fellowship in 2015 through a Delta Regional Authority pitch competition. His writing explores topics such as innovation, gratitude, failure, second chances, hard work, and how to see things from a unique perspective. This is his first book.

Williams grew up in Illinois, spent time in Southwest Missouri, and now calls Southeast Missouri home. He obsesses over pizza, enjoys playing chess, and recently began humiliating himself as a standup comedian. Find out more at smalltownbook.com.

www.ingramcontent.com/pod-product-compliance
Lightning Source LLC
Chambersburg PA
CBHW070658190326
41458CB00046B/6774/J